1 MONTH OF
FREE
READING

at

www.ForgottenBooks.com

By purchasing this book you are eligible for one month membership to ForgottenBooks.com, giving you unlimited access to our entire collection of over 1,000,000 titles via our web site and mobile apps.

To claim your free month visit:

www.forgottenbooks.com/free113455

ISBN 978-0-484-41893-5
PIBN 10113455

For support please visit www.forgottenbooks.com

O'er Oceans and Continents

WITH THE SETTING SUN

Blatter, George John

BY

FISCAR MARISON

THIRD SERIES

JERUSALEM, PALESTINE IN BEDOUIN GARB, SYRIA AND
THE ISLANDS OF THE MEDITERRANEAN,
SMYRNA, CONSTANTINOPLE,
ATHENS, CORFU

2750

CHICAGO
AUTHOR'S EDITION

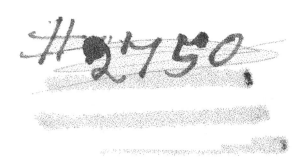

The Lakeside Press
R. R. DONNELLEY & SONS COMPANY
CHICAGO

PREFACE.

For this third series of "O'er Oceans" the author kindly requests a continuance of the good will which he met with in the publication of the first and second series. It is issued for the same purpose: to herald and promote the first English translation of the great Spanish work, "Ciudad de Dios."

FISCAR MARISON.

331 91ST STREET, CHICAGO.

LIST OF ILLUSTRATIONS.

CHAPTER I.

A Neat Piece of Smugglery — Ancient Jaffa —
Up Judea's Mountains to Jerusalem — At the
Austrian Hospice — Moonlight Wanderings —
An Hour at Gethsemane on Holy Thursday.

Having embarked on the steamer Thalia at Port Said,
we arose early next day, the Thursday of Holy Week, in
order to catch the first glimpse of the most sacred land
in all Christendom. The rays of the morning sun
blazed a wide pathway of glinting gold on the rippling
waves to the darker outlines of buildings and minarets of
ancient Jaffa, that rose on high bluffs over the blue
waters of the Mediterranean.

The steamer anchored in the deep water about a
quarter of a mile from the rocky shore, and in a moment the horde of carriers had surrounded the ship in
their boats and were climbing over the sides. Cook's
agent, who was dressed in a Turkish uniform, had
also boarded the ship with a bevy of carriers and boatmen to get his share of the spoils. I determined to
trust myself into his hands, and see what he could do for
me in my attempt to smuggle myself into Turkish territory without a visé. But another set of fiends had already
snatched our handbags. While I set about recovering
them from their hands by main force, I suddenly stood
face to face with Mr. Wiltzius, of Milwaukee, who was
having a similar scramble. Of course we had a hearty
handshake, and he immediately decided to join us in
Cook's boat. So, with a score of other passengers, we
were soon approaching the dangerous rocks that jut out
of the waters near the shore. Our stout Turk, who had

taken us in charge as Cook's agent in Jaffa, demanded our papers. He returned my American passport with the remark that it was not sufficient, and that I would have trouble at landing. We were now approaching the only opening between the broken rocks near the shore. Huge waves were rolling against them, and if the boatmen should allow the boat to swerve only a few feet to one side or the other, we would be dashed to pieces on their jagged edges. But they knew their business, and shot us through the passage on the crest of a wave, landing us safely at the pier of the custom-house. Our stout Turk simply pushed his way past the Turkish soldiers and custom officials, through a dark gateway, beckoning us all to follow. I was wondering where we would be stopped for our passports; but when we issued on one of the lively streets to Jaffa, I understood that our rotund guide had railroaded us through the whole crowd of venal officials by that open sesame of Turkish régime: bakshish. Well, it was a real service, and I scored it up in favor of Cook's agency.

From a distance at sea, Jaffa looks like a well-built city on the summit of wave-beaten cliffs. But when you pass through the narrow, ruinous streets, and see the hovels half buried in the wastes of thousands of years, you quickly change your opinion. The upper bazaars, and some few streets neighboring to them, show some signs of modern improvement and regard for cleanliness. They are full of life, and you will find people of all nations mixed up with the swarming Turks and Arabs. For those who are charitably inclined, it is better to procure some of the small coins, paras and metaliques, in order to satisfy the numerous demands of the beggars and bakshish hunters. We had made up our minds to stay for dinner in the Franciscan hospice, one of the oldest buildings in Jaffa and overlooking the beach. A brother showed us to Simon the Tanner's house, where St. Peter saw the clean and unclean animals which he was commanded to eat let down from heaven in a cloth. Through this vision he was instructed to receive the heathen centurion into the church, who was already waiting at the door of the house. A small mosque, very bare and dirty, stands on the place. The old man that had charge of it wanted us to take off our shoes; but as our shoes were much cleaner than the mosque we refused to undergo that trouble. There was nothing inside that we could not see from the door. It is of course only the traditional spot where Simon's house used to stand; for the house itself has disappeared long ago.

We came very near missing the afternoon train to Jerusalem by the blundering of Cook's agents that had charge of our baggage. Happily Mr. Wiltzius had bought tickets for us before we came. The train at first winds through the plains of Sharon, where the German Templars have planted some beautiful orange groves; but only for a few miles from Jaffa: beyond that the land is not much cultivated. The plows used by some of the natives on the fields were only two sticks of wood tied together at right angles. Cows or oxen are hitched to the free end of one stick. The plowman holds the upper end of the other stick and presses on the lower end slightly scratching the soil. After an hour or so we passed Ramleh, one of the larger villages along the railroad, where the old tower of Ramleh is visible from the train. Lydda comes next, which is the birthplace of St. George, and must have been quite a town formerly.

The progress of the train became still slower when we began to reach the mountains of Judea. They are a rocky desert, for the most part barren and treeless; yet wherever sheer necessity of procuring sustenance induced the natives to cover the rocky ledges with ground, and irrigate the sunburnt hillside, they were abundantly rewarded. Most of the time the train goes no faster than a walk. Such a pace would soon drive all traffic from an American railroad, but it seems to do very well in Palestine. Though the distance is only ninety kilometers or fifty-two miles, it took the train five hours to reach Jerusalem. The terminal station is outside the walls, southwest of the city. The different new establishments and settlements bid fair to become the most populous portion of the historic Jerusalem. Among the many establishments outside the city there are now quite a number of Catholic ones, such as the German hospice, the convent of Notre Dâme, the Crêche of the Sisters of Charity, St. Peter's Institute of P. Ratisbon for boys, St. Stephen's church and Dominican monastery, and the Assumptionists' hospice. We hired a carriage in order to be brought to Cook's office at the Jaffa gate. There I received a batch of welcome letters from home, reassuring me that all was well and prosperous. There are no wagon roads in Jerusalem, and therefore in order to reach the Austrian hospice, which was recommended by Mr. Wiltzius, it was necessary to pass again through the Jaffa gate on the road, which runs parallel to and outside of the west walls to the Damascus gate. Re-entering the city, we were soon hospitably quartered in the Austrian hospice.

I had made some plans of my own in regard to the use of the time after supper. I wanted to spend a part of the evening of Holy Thursday alone in the garden of Gethsemane, where our Saviour had begun his passion on the same night nineteen centuries ago. Perhaps the same beautiful moonlight filled the narrow streets and the valley of the Kedron when he so sorrowfully wended his way with the Apostles to the lonely garden. But my desire of being alone on this excursion was doomed to disappointment. I had hoped to be able to give my roommates the slip without being obliged to explain; but Mr. Wiltzius urged me to go with him to Casa Nova, the

Franciscan hospice, where he said we would meet Fathers V. H. and B. I thought this was a fine chance to steal a march on them, and I tried to induce him and my other companion to hunt up those two gentlemen without my company. But they would not be put off so easily as that. I had to reveal my intention of visiting Gethsemane, and then Mr. Wiltzius simply proposed to go with me. As for my other companion, who was so hard of hearing, he immediately suspected me of trying to shake him off for good, and leave him henceforth to shift for himself. It is needless to say that such a thought never entered my mind. I had given my promise to conduct him to Vienna, and nothing short of impossibility would ever have induced me to leave that promise unfulfilled. The trouble and annoyance caused by his infirmity, and his suspicions which are consequent upon it, were sometimes very great, as can easily be imagined. Of course after so much of my intended excursion had become known, there was nothing else to do than to invite my companions to join me.

There had been so much talk of the danger of passing alone through the streets of Jerusalem and the territory outside the walls, that the others insisted on taking along Ali, the kawass of the hospice. I had intended to go alone: now there was even a Mussulman in the party. The four of us sauntered through the narrow street leading to St. Stephen's gate, through the Turkish cemeteries, down to the torrent of Kedron, and over the stone bridge across it to the garden of Gethsemane. Its high stone walls, only a few paces from the Kedron, gleamed white in the moonlight, and the dark foliage of the olive trees that overtopped the walls were not stirred by even a breath of wind. To one side the rocky declivities of Mount Moria crowned by the spectral city walls, and on the other, the stony heights of Olivet guarded the intervening valley of Josaphat. Through this valley trickles the brook Kedron, downward to the Hill of Bad Council and Hinom Vale. What a sacred stillness reigned here on this night in these holy places! The silvery flood of moonlight lay poured out over hill and valley, over crumbling walls and dark olive trees, and over the gleaming rocks. Arriving at the low portal of the enclosure of Gethsemane, we saw several dark forms of persons crouched on the ledge of white rocks before the gate, seemingly on the same errand as we ourselves. The Franciscans are in possession of a part of the old garden of Gethsemane, and we expected some kind of divine service in it on Holy Thursday. So much the greater was our surprise to find the portals closely barred and our knocks remain unanswered. The rocks in front of the gate, mark the spot where the three Apostles fell asleep during the agony. About two or three hundred feet from the garden walls is the grotto, or rather the large cave, which is said to have been the scene of the bloody sweat of the Lord. As we were not familiar with the surroundings on our first night in Jerusalem, we did not visit the grotto until some days after. It may be that the Catholics had services there on that night; but we saw nobody going that way.

While we were contemplating the scenes around us, we noticed some people straggling slowly up the mountain along the road, and very soon we heard the mournful strains of a song, now and then interrupted by spoken words. Curiosity led us in the direction of the sounds, and we came upon about a score of people, very well dressed. They were standing on a ledge of the mountain listening to a Protestant preacher, who was reading St. John's account of this night's occurrences two thousand years ago. He seemed to be very solemn and sincere in his rendering of the passages, and the little band of pious souls sang with much affection and devoutness. Though it was only a Protestant service, the solemnity of the place and time no doubt was favorable to the workings of God's grace in the hearts of the participants. Those whom circumstances have deprived of the sunlight of true Catholic doctrine do well not to reject the pale glimmers of heresy for their devotion. We left these devout persons in order to meditate for a while near the entrance of the garden, and then returned across the Kedron, climbing up to the right around the city walls, to the Damascus gate on the other side of the city. Darkly the old walls and the crumbling battelments of Jerusalem rose, casting ghost-like yet well-defined shadows on the rocky, moonlit ground to our left. Nor did the Turkish sentinels that still watch the gates of Jerusalem deem it worth while to leave their dark recesses or molest us, as we passed under the vast arches of the Damascus gate. Only a short distance inside the walls, on a road branching off to the left, we soon regained our rooms in the Austrian hospice, and betook ourselves to our first night's rest in the Holy City.

CHAPTER II.

Good Friday on Golgotha — A Gathering From all Christendom — Turkish Coin, a Perpetuated Fraud — In the Footsteps of the Savior — "His Tomb Shall be Glorious."

Getting up early next morning we hastened on our way to the church of the Holy Sepulchre in order to take part in the service of Good Friday. Those parts of the church which belong to the Catholics are in charge of the Franciscans, who have been the guardians of the holy places in Palestine since the thirteenth century. Hence they also conducted the Latin services.

The church of the Holy Sepulchre on feast days will probably be a sad disappointment to the unwary stranger. In his own country he associates with the celebration of a feast in a Christian church, a solemn silence, devout postures of the people, and heart-stirring music. Here he will meet very little of all these. He will find the church of the Holy Sepulchre filled with motley crowds from all nations and climes, and belonging to different religions. At his very entrance his eyes encounter a guard of Turkish soldiers, lying or sitting on a raised platform, to the left and inside of the portals. They laugh and talk and gape at the passing crowds, even smoking their nargilehs. More of these Turkish soldiers fully armed, he will afterwards meet in all parts of the church, ready to interfere at any disturbance with their weapons. Then he will probably have to push his way through surging crowds of Russian, French, German, Austrian, and English pilgrims, and the adherents of the Greek, Coptic, Armenian schisms, who fill the spacious recesses and naves of the church. He can witness the services of the Latins, Greeks, Copts, and Armenians at stated hours of the day, sometimes at the Holy Sepulchre, sometimes at the chapels or altars belonging exclusively to each of these religions in different portions of the temple. Indescribable confusion often reigns, loud voices resound, songs of one language mingle with those of another. Now and then is heard the dull thud of the staff of a kawass, making way for some procession, or the clangor of arms, separating clashing factions.

It is providential that the almost impartial Turk, (impartial at least as long as the flow of bakshish is not lessened), has control of the holiest place on earth. Under present partial ownership of the church, among so many nations and factions, divine worship without this control would no doubt become entirely impossible on account of continued quarrels.

I took part in the Missa Præsanctificorum in company with the Franciscans and a goodly number of pilgrim priests. The robed and surpliced priests moved in procession past the Holy Sepulchre from the Latin sacristy up the stairs to mount Calvary in another part of the church. The exact spot where the Cross stood is in the hands of the Greek popes, and their fanaticism prevented any services being held on that altar. Immediately aside of it is the altar of the crucifixion—the spot on which Jesus was nailed to the Cross—and this is in possession of the Latin monks. The usual ceremonies of Good Friday took place according to the Latin rite. But the singing of the orations and lessons, and of the Passion was considerably mixed with Italian variations, which detracted a great deal from the beauty and the grandeur of the Gregorian chant. The solemn kissing of the large crucifix, which lay on the exact spot where the Son of God was nailed to the Cross, was performed by the priests, the nuns of the different convents, and by such of the pilgrims as were fortunate enough to be able to approach. These ceremonies, which typify the reality enacted on this spot, could not but deeply impress the beholder. Passing out of the ancient portals of the church into the square court or piazza, which is paved with large flagstones and surrounded by half-ruinous buildings, we had to take care not to step on the heaps of devotional articles exposed for sale in every direction. Near these gaudy piles of merchandise sat the venders and hawkers of different nationalties — Jews, Arabs, Armenians, Greeks, and Turks. In fact all the streets in the neighborhood are only a continuation of this motley bazaar. They charge what they can get, and seem to do thriving business. Buyers are always safer in offering about half of the price first asked. Money changers, brooding over their wire-screened boxes, sit around on every corner, ready to change your gold or foreign money into small Turkish currency. They take care to charge you enough for the exchange.

French or English silver or gold will serve very well for large payments of purchases, though even these are accepted only at a discount; but for daily use you must have Turkish money. This Turkish money is a grand scheme of larceny from the Sultan's throne down to the lowest beggar on the streets. Turkish money has different values according to the person you are dealing with, and according to the circumstances of the transaction. In dealing with the government its value is least; the wholesaler will accept it at a less value than the retailer, and the retailer will shrewdly gauge the value of the money he gets for his goods by the gullibility of the purchaser. Moreover, the same money has different values in different towns of Turkey. In its denominations it is the most illogical in existence. In Jerusalem, a medjid, which is a piece of silver about the size of our dollar, is equal to twenty-five piastres, each one of these is equal to nine metaliques and one kabach, one metalique is equal to four kabaches and two and a half paras. All below the ruba-medjid, or quarter of a medjid, is of a base alloy of copper and nickel, worth about one-hundredth of the face value. A bishlik is a thin piece of alloy an inch and a quarter in diameter, worth three piastres. As soon as you get outside of Jerusalem you will have to study a new table of values for your money. In fact you will find that your money changes its value as often as you leave the neighborhood of any considerable town in this land of bakshish and fraud.

After services we paid a visit to Casa Nova, and saw there our former fellow-travelers, Revs. B. and V. H. They had made a flying trip through India while Rev. S. and Mr. H. had gone direct from Colombo to Brindisi. The former two were to leave on the next day; they had been only two weeks in Palestine, and had not made the trip to Nazareth or other points in Galilee.

The dinner at the Austrian hospice was always a lengthy affair. To us it seemed unbearable, and very often we left the table before the others were half through. I suppose the slow and easy-going Austrians thought it rather strange. They indulged in great honneurs, when the Austrian consul came to dine.

In the afternoon of Good Friday the pilgrims and the resident Catholics turned out in great numbers to make the Way of the Cross on the Via Dolorosa publicly under the leadership of the Franciscans. At each station one of the Fathers, who wore a long, flowing beard, preached in French. The first station, where Jesus was condemned to death, is within a paved court, hemmed in by the walls of an old church and other buildings now used as barracks. The second, where Jesus took upon Himself the cross, is on the other side of the street, a little to the east of this court, where the Ecce Homo arch is built into the convent of the Ratisbon Sisters. The third, the first fall under the Cross, is on the same street in the united Armenian chapel. Adjoining the Austrian hospice, on a fork of the road, is the fourth station, the meeting of Jesus and Mary. The station of Simon is at the intersection of a road leading up to the church of the Holy Sepulchre; and that of Veronica is somewhat up the hill on this road, just before coming to the walls of the old city.

Going farther up the same road, beneath the maze of a dark, arched passage, on the other side of the ancient gateway, is the seventh station, the second fall of Jesus under the Cross. Within a Greek convent is the spot where the holy women stood weeping; it is marked by a cross in the outside wall of the convent bordering the street. The ninth, the third fall, is between the walls of the convent and the walls of the church of the Holy Sepulchre. The station of the despoiling of the garments is inside the church of the Holy Sepulchre, at the head of the stairs of the Latin chapel of the crucifixion. Only ten steps farther on, in the same chapel, Jesus was nailed to the cross, the spot being marked by a mosaic cross on the floor, which we had venerated that morning. The twelfth, the death of Jesus, is at the Greek altar of this chapel. The spot where Jesus died on His Cross belongs to the Greek monks, and is adorned by a magnificent bronze crucifix. It must be understood that the two altars, the Latin and the Greek, stand side by side in this chapel of the crucifixion on Mt. Golgotha. Between them is a space of about four feet. Near by, a statue of the Mater Dolorosa marks the thirteenth station. The fourteenth station, the burial of Jesus, is of course downstairs on the main floor inside the Holy Sepulchre.

Following the lead of the Franciscans, a multitude of earnest worshippers from all parts of the globe made the sorrowful Way. The whole courtyard of Pilate and the adjoining streets were filled with devout pilgrims, listening to the short exhortation and joining in the public prayers. The procession grew larger as it moved on from station to station. All were visibly moved and hesitated not to kneel in the filthy streets and join the responses. Conspicuous near the white-bearded Franciscan was always the tall and stout figure of Father V. H. seemingly more moved than the rest. The church was much too small for the crowds, and only a few could reach the last four stations. The services of the Latins on Good Friday night close with ten sermons, in ten different languages, held at the same time in the different portions of the church. During these days many colored lamps are lighted over the holy grave and in other parts of the basilica, so that the prophecy of the scriptures, that "his grave shall be glorious" is literally fulfilled.

CHAPTER III.

Bethlehem of Juda — Jaffa Gate and its Surroundings — The Cenacle — Cursed Hinom — Siloa's Pool in Josaphat Valley — Jealous Fanatics — A Spot of Ceaseless Wailing.

Early in the morning of Holy Saturday three of us were seated in a carriage on our way to Bethlehem. The drive to Bethlehem lasts little longer than an hour, and we soon alighted in the large square near the basilica of the Nativity. Thither we went while Mr. Wiltzius attended to some business at the rosary manufactories. The pealing of the great organ filled the church with gladsome strains of victory, and the Allelujas of the priests at the altar already announced the great triumph of the morrow. As we intended to visit Bethlehem more at leisure later we took only a cursory glance at the church and the caves of the Nativity. We were back in the city for dinner, and, having purchased Lievin's guide through the Holy Land, we started out on our visits to remarkable places in and about Jerusalem. Lievin, a Franciscan, has made a life-study of the holy places, and is by far the best and the most reliable author on Palestine. The Franciscans are in a position to speak with authority on holy places, since, as custodians, they are not only familiar with them, but are also likely to be cautious in interpreting the thousands of different traditions which exist among the Moslems, Greeks, Armenians, and Copts about the holy places. As for Baedecker's account, it is worthless wherever it pretends to treat of objects or traditions dear to Catholic travelers. I have more than once closed Baedecker's guide-books with disgust. This condemnation he deserves also in regard to holy places in other parts of the world.

We began our explorations at the Jaffa gate. This part of the city is the most frequented, for here is the business quarter of the Europeans inside of the walls. It is far from suggesting real European city life, for there are only a few modern buildings wedged in between old, crumbling walls and many native shops.

In Jerusalem one must get used to old walls, narrow, dirty streets without system or order. Those that wish to stop at a hotel will find one or two near the Jaffa gate, and there they will probably get little accommodation for much outlay. At the hospice, pilgrims find abundant fare, good advice, and moderate expense. Even if a pilgrim should not be able to pay, the monks would probably put up with that inconvenience, and let him depart in peace. Casa Nova is not far from the Jaffa gate, and in the immediate neighborbood of the principal object of interest — the church of the Holy Sepulchre.

Adjoining the Jaffa gate the old towers of Phasæl of David, and of Herod abutt on the city walls. They are used as Turkish barracks. In the tower of David, probably containing some of the oldest remaining walls of Jerusalem, is still shown the grated window near its square top, from which David is said to have cast lascivious glances at Uriah's wife at her toilet in an adjoining house. Here he is also believed to have sorrowed for his adultery with her, and to have composed many of the psalms. Passing along the street that runs southeast in front of these towers, we soon came upon the extensive Armenian convents, surrounded by large gardens. Within them are the sites of Annas' and Caiphas' houses, which are now replaced by Armenian chapels. The same street leads up to the gate of Sion, in a lonely and unfrequented part of the city. A narrow lane outside the walls passes by the plot of ground which the German Emperor recently presented to the Catholics of Jerusalem.

Some rods farther on stands the Coenaculum, where Christ held the Last Supper. It is a complex of old square buildings belonging to the Moslems, who, in their own fashion, likewise venerate some of the holy places sanctified by Christ. The hall of the Last Supper is on even ground in the largest of the ruinous buildings, and some of the stone seats and pillars are still shown as parts of the structure at the time of Christ. The hall is about fifty by thirty, entirely bare. At one end of it, up a short stairway, is the entrance to a smaller room, where a few dirty Moslems were squatting. Their faces were turned toward a dark grating which formed one side of the room. Behind the grating we could distinguish in the dark, a catafalque, or some such thing, covered with a black cloth. The ragged guardian of the place said that it was the tomb of David. Nobody believes it but the Moslems. Tombs are about the only things these Mussulmen venerate; they manage to have a great many tombs of all sorts of celebrities scattered over Palestine, but most of them need as much repair, and are as much neglected, as the silly Turkish traditions that they commemorate.

Leaving the Coenaculum we pursued our way across rocky, neglected paths, and miserable patches of plowed ground, along the walls of the city and down the steep hill toward Siloa's pool, almost at the bottom of the valley of Hinom. The Kedron here issues from the Josaphat valley, and its dried-out bed adjoins this pool of Siloa. This pool is formed by an embankment across the ravine stowing up the water which runs through secret channels from the city above. The old walls and buildings, which formerly encompassed this pool, were excavated some years ago by an English archæologist, and one of the buildings that came to light was an old Christian church. But the Moslems no sooner heard of the find than they claimed it as a former mosque, and they erected a small minaret over the restored church. The cavernous passage running up behind the church seems to be an old aqueduct.

On the slope of the opposite hill, which is a continuation of Mount Olivet, is the village of Siloam, the leper settlement. There the lepers of Jerusalem are quartered, for they are not allowed to reside in Jerusalem. They are governed by a sheik of their own, who distributes the precarious alms which they obtain from the city and which they beg during the day. Those that can yet move about are required to go begging. Numbers of them are seen lying in all stages of the dread disease on the road leading up to St. Stephen's gate, holding up their tin cups for alms to the passers-by. Very often I met these unfortunates on the road, and their pitiful moaning sounds yet in my ears. Some have purulent sores where the eyes ought to be, others have their mouth or nose eaten away, some hold up their horrid stumps of hands, from the festering flesh of which the bare bones protrude, others again show the ravages of leprosy on their exposed limbs. Most abjectly they lie along the roadside in the sun.

Passers-by dread giving them alms, for as soon as they give to one of them, the whole crowd will begin to gather around him, demanding, as of right, an equal gift. They seem to have little regard for one's fear of infection, and some will purposely seek contact with the clothes or hands of healthy persons, probably out of a secret desire to make others sharers of their disease. Some Sisters of Charity make regular visits to Siloam in order to do what good they can to the unfortunate sufferers.

In quite a roundabout way we clambered up the hill back to a place where the small postern gate of bab el

MOUNT MORIA, JERUSALEM, SEEN FROM MT. OLIVET

Mukraba pierces the city wall. Inside of this gate lies a large tract of waste land, covered with ruins, garbage, and sickly cactus plants. To our right in front of us stood some of the old temple walls on Mount Moria; to our left the Jewish quarters on Mount Sion. Having then reached the crumbling habitations, and the narrow, intricate lanes beyond this plot of waste land, we suddenly came upon some high portals, beyond which we were surprised to see a large open ground, covered with grass in some parts, not unlike a neglected park. It certainly is a rare sight in Jerusalem to see any kind of vegetation, for one meets nothing but crumbling walls, half inhabited ruins, dirty streets, and ragged inhabitants.

Hence we were not slow in pushing forward to enter the gates of this paradise. But no sooner had we attempted to set our foot inside than a shaggy Arab woman began to scream at the top of her voice. The first impulse of this dark fury was to rush at us, but on second thought she flew with disheveled hair and murderous screams into the arcades of the high walls to our right, and soon brought out a bevy of fierce Arabs, whom she harangued, making violent gestures towards us. We had unwittingly entered the Harem es Sherif, now the holy grounds of the Moslems, but formerly the ancient temple plateau of the Jews. Here on the site of the old Jewish temple stands the Omar mosque, which they esteem as little inferior to the one in Mecca, and on the southern end of the temple ground rises the mosque El Akseh, which is a vast basilica built by the crusaders on the site of Solomon's palaces. It would have meant nothing short of throwing our lives away to attempt entrance past the gathering crowd of fanatics. They eyed us with fierce, growing anger, and vented it in furious inprecation. We turned out of the passage, and soon came upon the Wailing Wall of the Jews, which had been really our objective point, and which we knew to be somewhere hereabout. It is a lonely place, where the ancient walls rise about thirty feet and overlook a waste of smaller ruins at their base.

A narrow passage has been cleared from encumbering ruins for about forty feet at the base of the great wall, so that one can approach the old foundation-stones, on which the newer wall is reared. There they stood, about twenty Jewish men and women, abjectly poor, leaning their faces against the huge foundation-stones, moaning and shedding tears in their loud prayers for the rebuilding of the temple, and the return of long past glory. It is indeed an indescribably sad sight to see the descendants of that chosen people, who had received this land from the Almighty helplessly wailing and sighing at those ruined walls. Vain regrets of a stubborn race, who heeded not the warnings of their God and their great prophet Jesus Christ, in the time of their visitation! When will they come to consider that He whose blood they had called down upon their heads and upon their children had overlookd this very wall from the heights of yonder Mount Olivet, and had shed as bitter tears as theirs at the ruins which He foresaw, and which they were now bewailing? There is not any better proof of the truth of the Christian religion in history than the existence to this day of the God repudiating and God-repudiated race, who then foreswore their Messiah and now, by their wailing and vain endeavors, proclaim the dire fulfillment of His prophecy. It is a consolation to know that the other prophecy will also be fulfilled before the end comes; namely, that the remnants of the house of Israel will be gathered into the one fold of Jesus Christ where they belong. So let them wail out their prayers leaning on these old walls; God will in time hear them, not in the way they now expect, but according to the magnitude of His mercy.

In the crevices of this wall many nails had been driven, for it is their custom to bring nails and drive them into this wall in order to induce the Lord to rebuild the temple. Some of them held up to us tin boxes for alms for the restoration of the temple, or perhaps for themselves.

Leaving this place of sorrow, we were surrounded by a bevy of children, in one of the narrow lanes, asking for bakshish. Only rapid flight will save the stranger from being swamped by crowds of these beggars, if he has been incautious enough to give alms to one of them in the presence of others. Towards evening, through many winding streets and bazaars, we found our way back to the Holy Sepulchre. Here good Father Joseph readily accommodated us in regard to the confession, which is necessary for the gaining of the indulgences of the pilgrimage. Afterwards we managed to worm our way into the interior of the Holy Sepulchre in spite of the immense crowds. But as the time allowed each one was so short as to preclude a closer inspection, I prefer to describe it later on. About midnight we went again to the Church of the Holy Sepulchre in order to be present at the midnight services. The whole vast interior was gloriously illumined by the multitude of colored lamps, especially around the grave. If the Franciscans, who are mostly Italians, had adhered more strictly to approved Gregorian chant, the solemnity of the occasion would have been much heightened.

We did not stay till the end of the Resurrection services, but after an hour or so we returned through the moonlit streets to the hospice.

CHAPTER IV.

EAST AND WEST IN JERUSALEM — ON MOUNT OLIVET —
AT THE GERMAN HOSPICE — IN CAVALCADE TO
EMMAUS — NEBI SAMOUIL AND KUBEBE — SIX
CENTURIES OF FRANCISCAN CUSTODIANSHIP.

I said my first Mass in the Holy Land on Easter
day, in the Latin chapel at the altar of the column of
the flagellation. Afterwards we strolled through the
neglected streets between the Damascus and the New
gate. Among the ruinous houses we found an Armenian
chapel dedicated to St. Cyprian.

Immediately adjoining the New gate, which is halfway between the Jaffa and the Damascus gate, is the
newly built institute of the Christian Brothers for Boys;
outside is the convent of the Sisters of Notre Dame, a
modern building. The porter of this convent invited us
to enter and look at the fine chapel; the front walls,
particularly in the sanctuary, are beautifully decorated
with Mosaics. The settlements of different nationalities, or rather of different religious denominations, are
in this neighborhood west of the city walls. These
buildings for religious and charitable purposes are mostly
of recent construction. The largest settlements are those
of the Russians and the Catholics. The Protestant
deaconesses conduct a hospital, and the German Templars, a religious colony coming from Wuertemberg, have
settled here and have large establishments. To the
south and to the north of the city, the territory is yet free
of settlements, but to the northeast on the summit of
Mount Olivet, the Russians have erected a large monastery and church. A separate tower, rising 200 feet above

the summit of the mount, commands the whole country far and wide. The Russian government, under the cloak of private enterprise of their Greek monks, has established its influence firmly in the whole of Palestine. Yearly pilgrimages from Russia are encouraged, and heavily subsidized by the government so as to familiarize thousands of the simple Russian peasants with the Holy Land. They return to their native country eager to see Russia obtain the lion's share in any future partition of Turkey by war. When once it shall become necessary, Russia will find no trouble in raising a mighty army for the conquest of the Holy Land. The Russian peasantry will rise as one man for such a crusade. Thus Russia shows herself by far the most shrewd and far-sighted among the European nations in regard to future Oriental spoils.

We did not proceed much farther just then, but returned to the hospice in order to await the visit of Revs. Blockmann and Rohde from Wisconsin, who had promised to make arrangements with us for to-morrow's trip to Emmaus; but after waiting a few hours in vain we again sallied forth, this time in an opposite direction, toward St. Stephen's gate. The street running past our hospice forms a direct thoroughfare northeast and southwest between the Damascus and the St. Stephen's gates.

Not far from the Austrian hospice on that road is the fine chapel of the Franciscans, erected on the spot where Jesus was scourged. Within the same grounds is also the place of the crowning with thorns. In the chapel of the flagellation several lamps burn continually. Connected with these sacred spots, in a convent near by, is also the novitiate of the Franciscans. Just before coming upon St. Stephen's gate, one meets the church of St. Anne, restored from the same stones of which the old church of the Crusaders had been built. The windows are of colored glass, very neatly fitted into stone frames. Under the main church is the crypt, where, according to the revelations of Mary of Agreda, the Virgin was conceived without sin. It consists of several chambers with altars, and the original bare rocks of the caves are still seen in some places. The rest of the rock is veneered with marble. Facing the church is the pool of Bethestha, under the vaults of an ancient church. It now resembles a spacious underground cavern half-filled with water. The large buildings neighboring to the church are the convent and seminary of the white Fathers, founded by Cardinal Lavigerie for the African missions.

One of the white-robed Fathers just then stepped out of the gate in order to give benediction of the Bl. Sacrament at the convent of the cloistered Carmelite Nuns on the summit of Mount Olivet. We gladly accepted his invitation to accompany him. Our way led us through St. Stephen's gate, down the hill to the ledge of rocks on which St. Stephen was stoned, and from there past Gethsemane up the hill. Near the summit stands the convent and church of the Pater Noster. They are a reconstruction of the buildings put up six hundred years ago by the Crusaders. Some of the foundation-walls date back even to the time of St. Helena. In fact, very few of the buildings and ruins commemorating noted places in Palestine are without traces of former structures, erected at the time of St. Helena in the fourth century, or at the time of the Crusades in the twelfth. Most of them, however, are buried many feet beneath debris and soil accumulations. We remained for benediction, and afterwards bought some mementoes from the very businesslike Sister that attends to the temporal affairs of the cloister. The others never leave the house, nor converse with anybody except through a thick, iron-spiked screen.

Their church is on the spot where our Lord taught the Our Father. Farther down the hill is another church, which commemorates the place where the apostles composed the creed, each one being moved by the Holy Ghost to pronounce one of the articles. From these heights the city of Jerusalem is seen spread out before the view. In the foreground, on the opposite heights of Moria, lies the temple plateau with the mosque of Omar, behind these a tangled, irregular maze of low, flat-roofed buildings. Most of them are ruinous, and small cupolas rise like hummocks above the flat part of the roofs. For in Palestine the roofs are mostly vaulted masonry, without any wooden beams. From the temple enclosure the old city walls zigzag around right and left to the tower of David on Mount Zion, peering above the farther side of the city. The circumference of the walls cannot be more than three or four miles, since an hour and half fully suffices for a walk around the whole city.

We returned to the hospice for supper, and afterwards followed the lead of Mr. Wiltzius to the German hospice outside the walls behind the Templar settlement. Some fifteen or sixteen priests from the United States were quartered there, being members of the German caravan from Cologne, making the tour of the Holy Land. Our intention was to make arrangements for accompanying the caravan to Emmaus on the morrow, the day just befitting such an excursion. Mr. Wiltzius, who had visited them that morning, got badly mixed up in his bearings. It was already dark as we passed through the Damascus gate, and instead of arriving at the German hospice, we came to the French consulate and to the Protestant hospital in another settlement. Though the deaconesses gave us very kind and explicit directions, we had great trouble to find the German hospice.

The members of the caravan were at supper, and the leader of it was just giving instructions regarding next day's excursion. We were invited for supper, and readily obtained their consent to make the trip to Emmaus with them. Mr. Wiltzius, however, and two of the priests had already become tired of Palestine life, and arranged to take the train back to Jaffa in the morning. The German hospice is an extensive building surrounded by fine gardens. All the guests seemed highly pleased with the accommodations. The only drawback they mentioned being the distance from the church of the Holy Sepulchre. The Austrian hospice, where we lodged, is only ten minutes' walk from that basilica, while Casa Nova, the Franciscan hospice, is in the immediate vicinity.

On Easter Monday I said Mass in the church of St. Anne near Stephen's gate, on the spot where the Mother of God was conceived without sin. I was afraid, of coming too late to start out with the caravan to Emmaus, but we arrived at the German hospice long before the party could be gotten ready. Most of them were not out of their beds. My companion and myself happened to get the sorriest nags of the cavalcade, and our saddles were of the clumsiest. My beast had a tender mouth, which the barbarous bridles of the Arabs had chafed into a bleeding sore. Nevertheless they plodded bravely on with the rest, over rolling stones and rugged ravines on the worn bridle-paths. To call the way to Emmaus a road, or even a decent trail, would not enter into the mind of the wildest mountaineers of the United States. It is nothing else than a succession of loose stones, rough rocks, and rain-worn water-courses, left to the wear and tear of many centuries. The same may be said of the roads I traveled afterwards alone to Naplouse. The horses stumbled on for an hour and half until we reached the summit of a high hill, crowned by a small mosque and a minaret. The Moslems call it Nebi Samouil, or tomb of Samuel. Inside the bare mosque, under a sort of alcove, is a wooden box covered with a pail, which the Mohammedans venerate as the grave of the great prophet Samuel. The ragged, bakshish-hunting keeper insisted on our taking off our shoes before entering; but most of the party were satisfied to look in through the door. From the top of the minaret we had a grand view of distant Jerusalem, Mount Olivet, the plains of Jericho, and the Dead Sea to the east. To the west glimmered the blue Mediterranean, and over the plains of Samaria to the northwest, the woody heights of Carmel intercepted the view of the seashore.

An hour's further rugged travel brought us to the gates of Kubebe, or Emmaus convent. In front of them stood a crowd of pilgrims who had come afoot, some Franciscan Fathers, and, glibly conversing with them, our eccentric fellow-passenger of the Britannia, Mr. Clark.

Beside the director of the caravan, we had a stout, Christian Turk as dragoman, whose family lived near the convent. He was a jolly soul, gorgeously fitted out in a kawass uniform. He insisted that the whole caravan should pay a visit to his wife and children. Before making a closer inspection of the convents, the director of the caravan also wished us to inspect the vineyards and other property bought here by the "Deutsche Palestina Verein." The object of the Palestina Society was to start colonies here and in some other places of the Holy Land. The director was full of enthusiasm, and tried to make us believe that Kubebe is an ideal site for a summer resort, and that the vineyards would bring large returns. They have converted the stony hillside into a vineyard, and planted a few fig trees; but the expenses have already exceeded by far the prospective gain. It certainly does not seem probable that they can induce colonists to settle here for any length of time, or that a summer resort will ever flourish in a rocky desert, without water and without shade. The Americans had but slight confidence in the success of the venture in spite of the enthusiasm of the director. So far the Franciscans are the only settlers. They have erected a spacious monastery on the foundation of an older one dating back to the time of the Crusaders, using it for a scholasticate for the education of their members.

Our caravan and the other pilgrims partook of a dinner in the large refectory of the Monks. There must have been some two hundred at the table. After dinner they scattered about the gardens and under the open cloisters, like a crowd of picnickers. Among them was a grey-headed German, who caused no small diversion by imitating the cries of all sorts of animals. All the guests of the good Fathers seemed to enjoy themselves very well. Mr. Clark, the defrocked Anglican minister, was already very intimate with one of the unsuspecting fathers. After resting for a while one of the Franciscans conducted the visitors to the remains of the church and convent built in the twelfth century. The excavations showed that they were extensive.

I may as well make mention of the zeal of the Franciscans in preserving and restoring the holy places in Palestine. Especially in the last half century has this pious work made progress in numerous places of the Holy Land. Only those somewhat acquainted with the run of affairs in Turkish countries can have a proper estimate of the difficulties to be encountered in such an undertaking. The Franciscans have withstood the persecution of six centuries, meeting not only the cruelty and rapacity of the Moslems, but the ceaseless stratagems of orthodox Greeks or Russians, Armenians, Copts, Jews, and Protestants, who pursue them with their envy and, by fair means or foul, try to come into possession of memorable places in charge of the Latins. The rights which the above-mentioned schismatics, heretics, and Turks claim in the church of the Holy Sepulchre, and in many other places, have been obtained entirely by intrigue and by confiscations, manipulated by influential partisans in government circles. Time and again the Franciscans have purchased locations, only to see them wrested from their hands as soon as they had erected their buildings, or find themselves forced to pay the purchase price over again as new Pashas came into power. That mere envy or avarice is the cause of these outrages is evident from the foul neglect and decay into which many holy places are allowed to fall after being wrested from the Catholics. Whereas the most pious care and devotion is everywhere seen in the holy places that are in the charge of the Latins, the contrary is often the case with those that are in other hands.

We asked Father Joseph, at the church of the Holy Sepulchre, (and he has spent there most of his life), why the great rotunda over the Tomb in that church was not kept in better repair. He told us that the Greek papas will not permit the Franciscans to make any repairs even at their own cost, and will rather let the church fall into ruins than co-operate with the Latins in restoring it. No doubt they are in hopes of obtaining sole proprietorship of the Holy Sepulchre in course of time. From all this it will be seen that the collections for the Holy Land, taken up every year all over the world, are very necessary and well applied. They enable the Franciscans and other religious orders to maintain the custody of holy places and reliable traditions about them. The Franciscans have certainly, in a special manner, earned the title of custodians of the Holy Land by their pious zeal during six centuries. Were it not for them it is doubtful, whether any vestige would remain of most of the holy places in Palestine.

Rested and well entertained, we again bestrode our horses and returned cityward on a different route. After climbing over a few hills, and following a trail over some fields past a ruinous village, we gained the Jaffa road. This is as fine a road as you would find anywhere. It was built for the retinue of the German Emperor, at the occasion of his visit four or five years ago. The same may be said also of the road to Jericho, to Bethlehem, and of the one from Haipha to Nazareth. To our left, as we followed the winding road to Jerusalem, we saw many of the foot-passengers straggling homeward from Emmaus over the hills and valleys. Long before we got to Jerusalem I suspect many of us gallant cavaliers were secretly wishing to exchange our chafing saddle-seats for the comfort of our empty chairs in the hospice. But not all of our spirit had as yet fled, for we made an attempt to gallop into Jerusalem in serried ranks of three abreast. However, the gallant onset ended in confusion long before the end of our journey, for instead of one or two blocks it was still nearly a mile to the hospice.

That evening after supper I wrote seventy-five postal cards, as greetings to friends at home.

CHAPTER V.

TANGLED STREETS — RUINS AND FILTH EVERYWHERE — PLANNING A RUSE ON THE BEDOUINS — PRISONERS OF THE HOLY SEPULCHRE — THE HOLY SACRIFICE AT THE MOST SACRED SHRINE ON EARTH.

Next day I had the privilege of reading Mass on the altar of the crucifixion on Mount Calvary. After bidding God-speed to Mr. Wiltzius, who that morning started on his return to Brindisi, we strolled out the Damascus gate to visit the caves or quarries of Solomon. These caves honeycomb the whole northwestern portion of Jerusalem. We preferred, however, to return into the city, and explore the corresponding quarter above ground. The streets are a puzzling tangle. A number of them are paved with cobble-stones, the steeper grades are terraced. A few are twelve feet wide, most of the others are much narrower; only two of them are wide enough to permit the passage of a wagon or carriage for a short distance. Sometimes a few of the more frequented streets are swept; outside streets are left in dirt and filth. Bazaars are only on four or five streets, principally in the neighborhood of the Church of the Holy Sepulchre. The other streets present a most desolate condition. No attempt at architectural beauty is visible, except on the new buildings of Europeans, of which there are not many in old Jerusalem. They do not indulge in front parlors in Jerusalem; the furniture in the houses of ordinary inhabitants are on a par with the outside of their habitations—a mat or two to lie on, a stone fireplace from which the smoke very often passes out through the vaulted ceiling or ruinous crevices.

The present Jerusalem is really only a collection of old walls and enclosures, still standing over the many layers of ruins piled up twenty feet above the original soil.

Bare, crumbling walls of old structures, without windows, and no visible doors, mere remnants precariously covered with a low roof, line the passages most of the way. Wherever a recess in the walls or an arched subway over the streets afford seclusion garbage and excrement litter the ground. This is especially the case where Turks or Jews inhabit. When I was told that cleanliness has much improved in the last ten years, I wondered how Jerusalem must have looked before that time.

I had some difficulty in getting a teskere or visé for my tour to Nazareth. I intended to make this tour alone, and in Arab or Bedouin garb. The sun had tanned my features considerably, and I was the proud owner of a stubby black beard; hence I thought that I could easily pass for an Arab sheik. Everybody maintained that a single European traveler would never pass the gauntlet of Bedouin nomads, as he was in danger of being held up and robbed even of his clothes. Why not steal a march on these marauders in their own guise? I asked. But all those to whom I mentioned my project thought this latter more preposterous and dangerous than the former, so that I had to keep it a secret until the time of my departure.

During the day we completed our purchase of a large number of articles as presents to friends in America. The native dealers made, or at least pretended to make, a large reduction on their price in view of doing business with Mr. Wiltzius, by whom we had been introduced on a former occasion. The devotional articles, especially rosaries, which are manufacured here and in Bethlehem in great quantities, seem cheap enough, but duty on them in the United States is proportionately heavy.

In order to celebrate Mass on the tomb of the Saviour, pilgrim priests must, as a rule, take lodging over night with the Franciscan Fathers in the Church of the Holy Sepulchre itself. All the doors of the church are locked by the Turkish guard at a certain hour of the night. The inmates, that is, the Latin and the Greek Monks attached to the church, are then prisoners until the Church is again opened in the morning. The opening of the Church of the Holy Sepulchre costs ten francs every time, and this sum is to be paid to a Turkish family by the different religious denominations, who request the opening of the church. It is easily understood, that on this account the Franciscans are most heavily bled, for the Latin pilgrims, who are the most numerous, must be oftenest accommodated. The Latin Monks have exclusive right of services every day until seven o'clock, after that the Greeks have their turn. But the Turkish soldiers will not admit even a priest before eight o'clock, the time set for opening the church. Hence the only alternative for a Catholic priest, who wishes to celebrate on the tomb of the Saviour, is to have himself locked up with the Franciscans over night.

We partook of the frugal supper, and were conducted to the cells upstairs. Father Joseph entertained us with a pleasant chat until we went to sleep, happy-prisoners of the Holy Sepulchre.

Early in the morning of the next day I had the happiness of celebrating Mass on the holiest and most remarkable spot on earth; for which all thanks be to Him who rested there in death, and who rose gloriously triumphant from this tomb. My companion entered with me into the low vault to serve my Mass, but the Franciscan Brother, seeing him rather unfamiliar with his duty as an acolyte, unceremoniously supplanted him at the offertory. Several women received holy communion at my hands through the low entrance of the Tomb. It was indeed a great privilege to offer up the great sacrifice on the very spot where the faith and hope of all Christendom was made certain.

PRACTICAL HINTS. In Jerusalem it is better to lodge in one of the hospices. The most convenient for those that wish to see something of Catholic services is the Casa Nova of the Franciscan or the Austrian hospice. The Brothers will also be of great assistance in procuring good guides, and in preventing exorbitant charges. The fare in these hospices is all that can be desired, and the remuneration asked is very moderate. Those that wish to see the holy places thoroughly should make a sort of outline or plan suited to the time of their stay, and to the amount of exertion they intend to undergo. Of course every one likes to take along some mementoes and relics of the Holy Land. For Catholics there is a vast assortment of rosaries, medals, crucifixes; these, blessed at the Holy Sepulchre and Bethlehem, will afterwards no doubt serve as the most valuable mementoes for their friends and themselves. The real value of such mementoes is often not realized until one is thousands of miles from the place where they were perhaps hastily obtained in the excitement of sight-seeing. But at home they will bring back the memory of strange surroundings and incidents of the time and place of their purchase.

IN ARAB COSTUME

CHAPTER VI.

In Bedouin Garb — A Bivouac on Judean Hills —
Roughing It — Causing a Scare — Beitin, Once
Bethel — Panic in a Harem — Luxuries of an
Arab Home.

After securing a teskere through the aid of the American consul, and procuring a Bedouin outfit through the help of Ali, our kawass of the hospice, I made preparations to leave alone and on foot for Nazareth. As I did not want to listen to any more discussion, the Arab clothes were smuggled into the porter's room by the help of Ali, and after dinner I arrayed myself as a Bedouin sheik for the journey. The under-garment is a long, sleeveless cotton shirt, reaching nearly to the heels. Over this is thrown an upper garment of striped material, and somewhat like a cassock, the two front flaps of which are buttoned only at the neck, and are held together in the middle by a sash. Over all this is thrown the haik, a loose mantle, with openings in the sides for the arms. The head covering is a tarbush, consisting of a large square kerchief with fringed edges. It is thrown over the head and fastened by a rope of camel's hair; this hair rope passes twice around the forehead and ends in long tassels behind.

As I was much sunburnt and had a black stubby beard, I could easily pass for a Bedouin sheik, so far as outward appearance was concerned. But the number of Arab words that I gloried in was closely allied to the minus. Ali did his best to enrich me. "Three words are sufficient," he said: "Salaam, aleikum, mafish." In other words; if I met any of the marauding nomads, and

47

felt like being beforehand in civility, I might say: "salaam"; or, if they first salaamed, I might answer: "aleikum." But if any of that scum of the desert should seek to enter into conversation with such a high-born chief as myself, they should be told to go about their business with a surly: "mafish." I found afterwards, that this three-cornered vocabulary, with its expressive bluff at the end, went far toward establishing tolerable relations between Arabia and America.

I started out early in the afternoon, intending to reach Ramallah about twelve miles to the north of Jerusalem. My traveling companion wanted to see me off safely for a few miles at least. But as we left Jerusalem from St. Stephen's gate, which is on the east side of the city, we at first pursued the wrong direction. It entailed an unnecessary climb of Mt. Scopus on the northeast of Jerusalem. After an hour and a half of climbing we found the right trail. Near a ruined village, whence the last view of Jerusalem could be had, my companion bade me God-speed, and I was launched alone on my ten day's trip.

Soon the difficulties of the journey became evident. I had taken along light shoes with thin soles. The northward trail was in some places a remnant of a road built by the Romans, which probably had not been repaired since their time. The large and small boulders had stood the wear and weather of two thousand years, and are now but loose heaps of stone. At other places the road was a mere trail full of holes and rugged edges. My shoes gave way in several places in a few hours; the thin soles were no protection against the rolling rocks and sharp projections.

I had left my partner not far from ancient Gibeon, the ruins of which are still traceable on the crest of a hill. Josua, when he came to exterminate all the inhabitants of Canaan, was neatly circumvented by the Gibeonites.

They sent an embassy, decked out in old clothes, on jaded and worn beasts, in order to make him believe they had come from a great distance outside the limits of the doomed country. Yet they were only twenty miles from Jericho, where Josua was encamped. They began to flatter him with the great things they had heard of the Israelites, thereby securing a treaty, which Josua confirmed with an oath. When the Israelites a short time afterwards found that these people were living right in the midst of the promised land, they did not dare to destroy them on account of the oath. So the race of Gibeonites was allowed to live as slaves ever afterwards, to be employed as menials at the temple.

Past Gibeon, a sloping plain stretched away to some rugged hills in the distance. The lingering sun's rays still rested on their rocky crests. Behind them I had been told to look for Ramallah. In the valley I met a few shepherds and wandering Arabs, who surveyed me with inquisitive looks. The shades of evening were lengthening over the slopes. On the hillsides roughly-clad shepherds were gently urging their flocks homeward, and from a great distance the cheery voices of children resounded. I traversed the plain and climbed around rocky bluffs, and yet no Ramallah hove in sight. Darkness overtook me still groping over the loose rocks of the indistinct trail, but the faint barking of dogs drew me on to continue my search in the nightly gloom. There are no habitations of any kind in Palestine outside the villages. A farmhouse is altogether unknown. After wearily stumbling onward for a half an hour or more, the barking sounded fainter than before. I began to familiarize myself with the prospect of sleeping on the rugged hillside, just as ages ago the patriarch Jacob had done not far from this very neighborhood.

The trail having soon become undiscernible, I sought for some sheltering hollow in rocks for protection against the chill wind that blew across the hilltops, and, wrapping myself in the wide haik, laid down near the roadside to sleep. But the wind became still more chilly, and forced me to seek the lee side of a stony ledge on the other side of the trail. It was a mighty hard bed, but I was tired and I sank into a fitful doze as the moon began to rise over the hills. Not a soul had I met on the way since sunset, and the region seemed altogether deserted. The voices of the night in other countries, such as the chirping of crickets, the tremulous notes of the frogs, which softly lull to sleep on the prairies or in the woods of America, are not heard in these hills of Judea. The soundless night broods as if in speechless sorrow over the stony regions that repudiated the Savior.

The moon had climbed high up the starry vault, when suddenly I was awakened by the sound of many voices coming over the hill behind me. Peering over the top of the stone ledge, I saw about twenty of the natives, or Arabs, rapidly coming down the stony trail, which gleamed in the bright moonlight, within a few paces of where I lay. Naturally the appearance of a band of Bedouins so late at night, and in a region which I thought uninhabited, gave rise to some uneasiness. At any rate they would wonder much to find a lonely wanderer out on the hills, and their curiosity would be annoying. I therefore crouched in the shade of the rocks, covering myself with the black haik. They would probably pass by without seeing me, unless they had a dog with them. Laughing and chattering they stumbled past, so close to me that the shadow of some of them, and of an ass which they were driving, fell upon the white rocks near me. None of them noticed me, and they disappeared down in the valley around another hill. When their voices had become inaudible I arose and sought for a more quiet resting-place some rods inward from the road, for they would surely see me in my old place, if they should happen to come back the same way. I was not wrong in my conjecture about their return; in half an hour I heard their voices again approaching. All of them, however, dragged up the rocky trail, unsuspicious of the presence of their white brother bivouacking on the hillside.

I was not further disturbed that night, though I could get only fitful dozes of sleep, while the half disk of the moonlight slowly ran its course across the heavens. The edges of the rocks on which I lay would not accommodate themselves to my aching limbs. This bivoucking under the sky was very pleasant — that is, to read about, or to muse about afterwards. But sometimes doubts will insinuate themselves while one revels in the reality. However, it might have been worse, and I was somewhat surprised at last when I woke up and saw that dawn had encroached upon the moonlight. Natives were now coming down over the hill in groups, driving some asses. After they had passed on to the valley I got up to make my toilet. It consisted merely in leisurely arranging my sash and my haik, and readjusting the tarbush. While I was thus engaged a solitary camel-driver was slowly urging his beast over the hilltop; coming nearer, and raising his eyes toward me, he stood like one petrified. A black figure, half seen over the projecting rocks, and so deliberately fumbling around his waist, must have seemed to him very suspicious. No doubt he thought I was but a leader of a gang of Bedouins, concealed behind the rocks, ready to rob him of his only possession. When now I with equal deliberation moved up toward the road, I saw him nervously clutching his club tighter and in a frightened tone, asking a question. Not knowing how many might be in his wake, I passed him on the trail, with a surly "ma-fish." This was somewhat of a superflous admonition, for he seemed only too glad to "go about his business." Curious to find out whence the barking of the dogs last evening had proceeded, I pursued the trail and found a ruinous gathering of old walls on the top of a hill only one and a half mile farther on. But the roads were so rugged that I was not sorry for having bivouacked under the sky. Moreover, I found that it was not Ramallah, but the remains of some ancient walls, inhabited by a few furtive Arabs. They now glared at me in no friendly manner, out of their dark holes.

I hastened on in the probable direction of Beitin, or ancient Bethel. Even so early in the day my feet began to pain and swell from the roughness of the road, and every step soon became a torture. I began to realize what fatigue and labor Jesus Christ must have undergone in his continual wanderings, very often barefooted, as tradition tells, up and down the land of Israel. I do not suppose that these roads were any better in his time. No wonder he sat weary at Jacob's Well. The trail led gradually down into a valley, where there seemed to be better soil. A spring irrigated it, and two or three plowmen were scratching the ground, urging on their beasts of draft with continual calls. Suddenly I heard the clatter of horses' hoofs on the stony trail behind me. A European came down the hill, preceded by a soldier in dirty uniform and a mule-driver; the three of them were armed to the teeth, and were dragging along a mule laden with goods. Muffled in my haik I stood at the roadside to watch their passing. They eyed me suspiciously from afar, prodded their beast into a furious gallop past my standpoint into the rocky ravine ahead, and disappeared behind the cliffs in the valley below. Why should they be afraid of a single man on their road, and he only a counterfeit sheik?

My only breakfast was a not very cool drink from the perturbed water of a spring below. By this time I had slowly reached the rocky wilderness of the next hill.

I looked anxiously for Beitin. In vain, however. Only after two hours more of weary climbing I reached the scanty fig orchards on its outskirts.

But when I came to its ruinous walls, scattered without any order about the crest of the hill, and saw the dung piles around them, the garbage and offal littering the passages, my hopes of refreshment and rest began to wane. Nobody was to be seen, no sound issued from the crumbling holes in the walls that served as doors, only a penetrating stench of burning dung filled the air. In vain did I look for a bazaar, or for a likely place to get something to eat. At length I met an old man, who was carrying a child on his arm. After repeating to him the word "khan, khan," with many an expressive gesture toward my mouth, he pointed to a ruin near by. I found that it was a cavernous vault, seemingly the foundations of a ruined building. The whole front of the vault was open, and the inside was entirely bare except a few stones in the dim background to serve as a fireplace. Four or five dusky Arabs were lying or sitting on the bare ground. One of them, tall and gaunt, more bandit-like than the rest, came from the rear, and understanding from my signs that I wanted something to eat, he, in equally expressive signs, requested "bakshish." It looked highly problematical whether he had any food to give. There was none in sight, and he seemed to be very hungry himself. So I was not particularly forward in obliging him with any of my loose change. The other inmates jumped up from their mats and surrounded me. My haik was a new one with thin red stripes along the seams; it took their fancy by storm. All seized hold of it, and began to examine it with greedy eyes. With the air of a sheik of thousand lances, I wrenched it from their grasp, almost tearing it, and turned away with an angry "mafish." That word seemed to have the same effect with those people as the sight of an American man of war in the harbor of some Turkish port. Ali had given me the most useful and the most necessary word in the whole Arabic language. They did not follow me as I turned another passage between the ruins.

There I met the old man with the child again, and made more signs for something to eat. This time I enforced them by showing a ruba-medjid, or a quarter of a medjid. It is a silver piece of the size of our quarter. He led me to a hole in the wall. It was the entrance to a small courtyard, surrounded on the other three sides by the ruinous walls of low huts. These had no windows, only three or four dark apertures. The yard was strewn with big boulders, which could be used as stepping-stones over the reeking dung and mud. Some pigs and goats groped around, three or four women and some children, only half dressed, stared at me in the hot sunshine. One of them was seated on one of the stones kneading a mass of dough on a flat piece of board on the ground. The dough looked almost as black as herself, for every now and then as she turned it, an end of it flopped into the dirt of the yard.

Another woman sat swinging a goatskin full of milk, suspended from a peg in the wall. As she pushed it from her, a drop or two of the milk would gurgle out of legs of the goatskin. In a corner a mother sat, nursing an infant at her bare breast. The fourth one came close up to me to satisfy her curiosity about my new haik and striped undergarment. All the while the old man stood by scowling at the women, who probably were his daughters-in-law. How could they thus allow a stranger to look on their unprotected faces? These were probably his thoughts. But he need not have worried. Their beauty was more witch-like than bewitching. Desperately I held out the silver coin and pointed to my open mouth.

But to my signs and motions they answered only by

loud laughter and chatter among themselves. A boy of fourteen, dressed only in a dirty shirt, entered fully into the fun of the situation, laughing and talking with them and stretching out his hands for my ruba. When I thought they had comprehended my meaning, I gave him the quarter. He and one of the women rushed with it into one of the holes, and I thought the problem of providing for an empty stomach was to be speedily solved. But they soon returned empty-handed, and, it seemed, for new frolic. I grabbed the youngster by the neck and threateningly raised my cane. Tableau: Shrieks from the whole chorus, the boy tearing away, running into the hut, and bringing back the coin. I had accidentally heard the word fig in Arabic and kept repeating it, while again offering the coin. Finally one of the women climbed over the top of a wall and brought a wooden dish full of figs, while the boy had fetched something like pancakes. The dirt on the figs immediately suggested the handling they had undergone in the unwashed fingers of these women, while the pancakes were undoubtedly baked from the same kind of dough that one of these women had kneaded on the filthy courtyard ground.

As he saw me hesitate, the boy eagerly tried to convince me of its being eatable, and began to tug at the rubber-like black mass, gulping it down in great chunks. I left him to enjoy his banquet and began to fill my sash with handfuls of the figs. But though they would probably have gladly sold the whole outfit for a few paras, the boy tried to stop me from taking more than two handfuls for the ruba-medjid. Several times during these transactions the old man had already interfered and waved back the old hags; but now, since the coin was secured, he gave me to understand that I must depart immediately. He probably thought that the harem of his absent son or son-in-law was sufficiently demoralized, and that the line must be drawn somewhere. That old Moslem probably will never know with what a relieved and lightened heart the counterfeit sheik issued from the stench and filth of his son's harem. As I pursued my way through the reeking and filthy ruins of Beitin, it was hard to realize that this was ancient Bethel, the place where the angel had descended on a ladder from heaven to our sleeping forefather Jacob, and where he had set up the anointed stone to commemorate the great promises he there had received from the Lord.

CHAPTER VII.

In the "Valley of the Robbers" — Shadowed — Suspicious Company — My Own Jailer — A Sleepless Night.

I slowly pursued my way down the hill, eating of the dried figs. The road did not improve but rather got worse, and the hill was very steep. About a mile down the valley I came to a cistern. While sitting there a group of Arabs gathered around it, eyeing me curiously and seeking to enter into a conversation. Two or three of them were armed with long brass-bound carbines. A few girls also came to draw water in their earthen jugs, which they placed on their heads and carried all the way up the rugged path to Beitin. Two of the men were mule-drivers, and one of them was armed with a gun. As I wanted to drink, I had to ask for their jug, and so revealed my inability to speak Arabic. This seemed to make them more bold, and I thought it best to move on after I had satisfied my thirst at the brackish cistern. But I soon noticed that they were following at a distance, dodging my footsteps up and down the rugged hills, past olive patches on the hillsides and the ruins of a village farther on. There they apparently joined a long pack-train of mules which was wending its crooked way through the ravine.

The valley does justice to its name, at least in outward appearance, for it is a long defile between two rocky declivities. By this time the soles of my shoes had become completely worn through by the rocks, and I could not move a step without the greatest pain. My feet were painfully swollen. Nevertheless I pushed forward, down the valley to a place where I found water trickling from the rocks. It goes by the name of Robbers' Fountain. Glad to be free from the suspicious company, I slaked my thirst and stretched out on the soft grass for a rest. But I was soon disturbed. At some distance in the rear I again saw the armed muleteer slowly jogging along the trail, and not far behind him his partner with two jackasses. In the dried-out bed of a torrent below now and then bobbed up the head of another man whom I had not seen before. Any sign of suspicion at such extraordinary movements would have been a great encouragement to any evil designs they might have. Therefore I pretended to take the utmost ease, and simply watched the man with the gun as he passed reluctantly by. He probably did not know what to make of the unperturbed gaze with which I eyed him as he passed, and if the trio had any plans they must have been disconcerted. A few rods onward he threw himself under a tree, allowing the driver and his ragged partner in the ravine to come up with him. There they lay, seemingly resting by the roadside. I rose after a little while and slowly proceeded on my way, too footsore to go even at an ordinary pace. They allowed me to pass, but soon afterwards came up.

I saw that I could not avoid some kind of intercourse, and therefore determined to be beforehand. I wanted to reach Naplouse, or Sichem, but had no knowledge of its whereabouts or its distance. My feet would hardly carry me a mile farther What if I could get the use of one of their beasts? Even if their intentions were evil, I would be better off with one of their asses in my possession. I resolved to get possession of a mule and ward off treachery later. I gave them to understand that I would pay a ruba-medjid, not wishing to let them perceive how anxious I was to procure a beast at any price. The shining quarter immediately took their eye; a second one, drawn from my haik, secured the larger of the two asses. What a luxury! To be carried along on the back of that beast, while my aching feet dangled down at leisure, untouched by the rough ground. I resolved to make use of that animal and its drivers as long as possible, whether they were bandits or not. Soon the trio held a conference, whereupon one of them began to urge my mule briskly forward, slashing it across the ears, poking it from behind, and accompanying his cuff with such unceasing sounds as hm, brr, rr, ghee, ss. The man with the gun and his ragged partner with the other mule were soon left behind. At frequent intervals my driver made signs and motions for additional bakshish. This happened especially when we had to overcome bad stretches of the road, so that in the course of an hour I had already raised the quarter medjid to a whole one. I insisted, however, on not paying him until the end of the journey.

After leaving the Valley of the Robbers, we passed the trail leading to Siloe, where Heli and Samuel guarded the Sanctuary of Israel before the temple was built in Jerusalem. Soon we came to a rugged hill over which the ass could not carry me. To walk even these short distances was a torture, and I realized that these Arabs, whatever was their ultimate intention, were a godsend to me at present. From the top of the hill I surveyed a wide valley, bounded by the mountain of Gilboa. Long before I could drag myself across the declivity my driver had arrived on the other side with the beast, and stood talking to the keeper of Louban khan. The khan was but a thatched roof, resting on two ruined walls. The sinister keeper invited me to stay, but the bare ground and few straw mats were no temptation, and I preferred the ass's back to the suspicious hospitality of the swarthy host. So we pushed on across the plain, seemingly to a large town at the foot of the Gilboa Mountains in the distance. The evening sun lay spread over the landscape, and intervening clouds now and then sent vast shadow-patches over the green valley and distant mountain slopes.

Not far away in the valley our trail divided into two branches; one to the left to a large town at the foot of a mountain, the other to the right toward rugged hill country. My driver suddenly stopped and peremptorily demanded a medjid. I gave him to understand that he would get it as soon as we would come to Naplouse. As he would not acquiesce, and as I would not willingly have relinquished my seat for ten medjid, I gave him a half medjid. Even this was a mistake, for now be began to protest, as I thought, that Naplouse was too far away and he would bring me to a better lodging for the night. I was half amused at his protests; he was certainly unwilling to go as far as Naplouse, therefore he drove the ass into the side trail to the right. It led to the foot of a considerable hill, to the top of which he kept pointing. As we reached its base we met several Bedouins with their long shafted and brass-bound carbines sitting or standing in the ravines on both sides of the path. My driver exchanged a few words with them, but my desire for rest and refreshment now was stronger than all suspicions. Besides it was time enough to look for the defense when there was any sign of attack.

The sun was sinking, and its last rays were falling on a cluster of ruinous walls crowning the heights before us. To ride up the rugged trail was out of question, and this last half hour of climbing was probably the most painful half mile I ever traveled. My feet were fearfully swollen and bruised by two days' travel on the rugged trails. Up the hills and through the stench of burning excrements, which are used for precarious fuel in these countries, he led me to an enclosure surrounded by ruined walls. A few ugly old women, some dirty children, a starving dog, several goats and sheep, and even a cow were stumbling over the boulders that projected like islands out of the mud and manure of the small yard.

But I cared not for all that. I sat down on one of the stones near the entrance and began to take off what was left of my footwear, demanding fresh water with the air of a pasha. I suspected that pouring water over my burning feet was probably the greatest luxury I would ever obtain in such a place as this. I was not mistaken. While I sat cooling my feet with the water which the women brought to me in a tin can, my mule-driver stood conferring with one of the old women. My pantomimes to procure something to eat seemed to make no impression. But he beckoned me to a low door in the old wall, leading into what appeared to be the vault of an old ruin with an arched roof. A round hole in the rear wall was the only window. On the bare ground in the middle was spread a mat, around it I saw all kinds of rubbish and implements littering the corners. My host pointed to the mat, and I understood that it would be my couch for the night.

I began to long for the stony resting-place of last night, but I was too tired to think much of looking for one on the outskirts of the mountain just now; besides I was still in a faint hope of getting something to eat. So I at once lay down on the mat with a bag of some kind of grain for a pillow. After a while in came the Arab with a roll of the pancake, such as I had seen at noontime in Beitin, a can of water, a small tin cup with ill-smelling salve, and a hard-boiled egg. Stretching himself out at my side in full length, he gave me the egg and offered me some of the black tough pancake. Seeing that I hesitated to eat, he wrenched off big pieces from the rubbery substance, and dipping it into the dirty salve began to chew away at it with immense gusto. In order not to despise his hospitality altogether, I yielded to his urgent invitations. But the dirt and the toughness of the bread, and the smell of the grease prevented me from swallowing any of it. I contented myself with the single egg and the stale water. Having finished this repulsive meal, I tried to make my swarthy host understand that I must have a light of some kind. Whereupon he returned with a tiny kerosene torch lamp, which could contain only two or three thimblefuls of oil. My suspicions were aroused again when I saw standing in the doorway be hind him his afternoon companion, fumbling with his brass-bound carbine, and grinning over the shoulders of the ass-driver. When they were about to leave I saw them produce a ponderous key and insert it into the plank door on its outside. Did they intend to lock me in this hole over night? In spite of my weariness I jumped up before they could draw the rickety door toward them and turn the rusty bolts. With an angry "mafish" I hurled the ass-driver out of the doorway against his mate, and wrenched the key from the lock. In strong English I told them that "if there was any locking to be done, I was the one to do it, and from the inside." They seemed to be paralyzed by the proceeding. But that made no difference to me, angry as I was. I slammed the door before their faces and locked it from the inside, storing away the ponderous key under my pillow. I could at least keep undesirable company out, even if their intention was to detain me as desirable company within. I heard them rummaging around and talking in a low voice for a while on the outside, while I made preparation to sleep and leave the rest to Providence. Entrapped or not, I was too tired to think of much more than rest and sleep.

But in spite of my fatigue I scarcely obtained a half hour of sleep during the night. Outside was the bustle of men and beasts retiring to rest. Inside was the stuffy air, the hard couch, and a bloodthirsty host of mosquitoes beginning their wrathful music around my ears. The haïk, thrown over my head, was no protection against them, for they managed to find an opening no matter how I adjusted it. As the noise on the outside gradually subsided, the music of the ravenous insects became so much the louder, and, in unison with it, a mysterious crackling noise sounded from some dark corner behind me, as if someone were slowly breaking through the walls. From another quarter a stealthy cackling, as if from a disturbed chicken-roost, joined in the hideous concert.

It had been too dark when I entered this chamber of horrors to see anything except the mat and the immediate surroundings. I lighted the small torch and groped around to examine the lair. It was a cavern about nine feet square vaulted over by solid masonry. Brushwood lay heaped up in one corner, an old plow in another, bags filled with grain of some kind stood at the head of my resting-place, broken implements near the door. From the rough vault hung down long strings of dusty cobwebs, and the moonlight gleamed through the chinks of the plank door. I could find nothing to explain the noises, for they had ceased as soon as I lighted the lamp. One of them was satisfactorily explained soon after I extinguished the light; a rat ran over my legs, and being satisfied of that at least, I began grimly to enjoy fitful dozes of sleep. The mosquitoes had a high time of it that night, as far as I could judge from their satanic music. On account of the unbearable closeness and stench of the air I could not keep the haïk over my face for more than a few minutes. I wondered afterwards why the thought of leaving the cavernous quarters never came to me. It must have been on account of the extreme fatigue.

The dawn at length began to glimmer through the joints of the door, and I heard the noise of awakening men and animals. The suspicious behavior of my hosts yesterday was still fresh in my mind, and I somewhat apprehended trouble at my departure. However I soon found that if they had meditated any treachery, they must have changed their minds, for when I unbolted the door I found no obstacle, and an old woman standing in the yard readily showed me the way out to the hillside, where my ass-driver and a dozen of other Arabs were sitting on the detached rocks, or standing on the scanty grass. I bargained for an ass to ride to Naplouse and for a pair of their shoes. As for breakfast, they looked hungry enough themselves to cause doubt whether they had any to spare. My ass-driver of yesterday grinningly sold me his shoes. They were merely thick soles of raw cowhide, ending in a peak over the toes. The top was thin red leather latched with heavy leather strips. He took what was left of my old shoes away with him, and came back leading the mule I had bargained for. We were soon on the way, and out of sheer hunger I found myself munching some of the dirty pancake of which he was making his breakfast. No wonder: I had not had anything to eat for almost two days, except a few figs and the hard-boiled egg last night.

CHAPTER VIII.

At Jacob's Well — Fanatical Naplouse — Gal-
loping over Morasses — Daoud's Anxiety —
Welcome Hospitality — On the Plains of
Esdrelon.

The sun was just rising over the eastern hills, casting
long shadows into the wide valley of Sichem, to which we
were now descending. We traversed it in about two
hours, and came to the foot of Mount Garizim, where the
ruins of Jacob's Well still stand within an enclosure. My
driver had continually asked for increased and immediate
pay during the whole time, but I was firm and told him
he would get it in Naplouse. Sulkily he waited on the
road while I went to see the old well of Jacob. An old
man unlocked the gate of the enclosure, and conducted
me to the ruins of a church built over the well by the crusaders. Under a vault of these ruins is the opening of
the well. Its top is lined with stones that looked old and
worn enough to have been in use at the time of Jacob.
Grooves several inches deep were worn into them by the
ropes with which the water was drawn. The old man let
down a triple candle light into the circular shaft, which
illumined the sides and the bottom of the well a hundred
feet below. Its springs were now dried up. Here Jesus
sat, tired and hungry, burning with the desire of bringing
erring men back to his truth. Here his divine affability
converted the Samaritan woman and the inhabitants of
the neighboring city.

We resumed our way along the foot of Mount Garizim
and soon entered the narrow valley between it and Mount
Hebal to the left. Naplouse, the ancient Sichem, lies

crouched between these two mountains. On Garizim the Samaritans had their temple, and the inhabitants of Naplouse still resort to its summit as a holy place. To the right, at the foot of Hebal, is the tomb of Joseph. Both it and the well are in the hands of the Greeks or Russians. We passed many barracks and many Turkish soldiers, for Naplouse is quite a town. The Moslems here are very fanatical, and often molest Christians passing through. None of the guards however troubled me, for I was for the time a free and roving Bedouin. Nor was I molested in any way in the streets of Naplouse. My ass-driver got several additions to his pay by dint of continual demands. After some fruitless inquiry about the Latin church I found a shop-keeper who spoke Italian, and sent a boy to show us the way. There the ass-driver left me to my fate. He probably had more ready cash in his hands than he ever expected to get, and no doubt had a good time on that day. There are only a few Latin Christians in Naplouse. They have a chapel attended by an Italian priest. The servant received me at once without distrust into the house, but I had some difficulties in making the padre believe that I was a Catholic priest. I always found Italians somewhat suspicious in that regard. They often asked me why I did not wear a cassock while traveling. A very practical idea, I must say, to go around the world in a cassock! But they stick to forms. Of course we must excuse the good Father in Naplouse; others besides he would have hesitated to believe that a priest was hidden under my Bedouin outfit. But I soon managed to overcome his distrust, and then he treated me quite hospitably.

I was completely worn out. Somewhat fearing an attack of fever, I took a dose of quinine and went to bed. In the meanwhile my host promised to procure a horse and a moukar for my journey to Nazareth. When he

called me to partake of some dinner there was a country-
man of his at the table with him, and we managed with
some difficulty to make ourselves understood. Gladly
paying for his services, I bade good-by to the Father and
mounted the horse which had been brought by Daoud,
a Christian moukar. He was a short chunky Arab, and
rode a small mule. What a difference there was between
the Moslem Arabs of yesterday, and this Christian
moukar of to-day! Though of the same station and condition of life, he was a civilized man, had good manners,
whereas the former were little less than savages. Not
once on the road did he refer to the wages I had promised
him, nor to any extra bakshish.

The valley between Mount Garizim and Mount Hebal
is narrow. Naplouse, being a large town, extends
through this valley for about a mile. There are still some
descendants of the ancient Sichemites, and in their house
of worship they show the most ancient manuscript of
the five books of Moses extant. It is in the form of a
scroll, which runs on two rollers, like the liturgical books
of the Jews in their synagogues of our day. The five
books of Moses are the only scriptures these Sichemites
recognize as inspired. The name Naplouse stands for
Neapolis, the name given to Sichem by the Romans
after the time of our Savior. The main street of Naplouse, following the course of the valley and intersecting
the town through its whole length, is one continued
bazaar where much native business is transacted. The
rest of the town has the usual ruinous and neglected
appearance common to all Palestine. To look for grand
buildings or decent dwellings would be useless. The
crumbling walls of ruins, covered with thatched roofs,
furnish habitation to the majority of the population.
The filth in the streets is, it seems, more abundant
than in Jerusalem.

After traversing the valley of Sichem, Daoud took

a trail to the right up the mountainside. He was no laggard, and continually prodded his mule onward, urging me to make haste. The sun shone warm on the mountains, several of which we had left behind, when Sebastieh, the ancient capital of Samaria, on the top of a high hill, came to view. There are many ruins on its outskirts. The trail had become more passable after we left Naplouse, and the country showed more signs of vegetation. We passed several fine springs, and much of the land was under cultivation, or covered with olive and fruit trees. Proceeding some seven or eight miles of hilly country beyond Sebastieh, we entered a wide plain, across which we saw Bethulia perched on a conical shaped hill to our left. This hill rose from the plain, and was somewhat detached from the other mountains that encircled the plain of Bethulia. Holofernes had a fine camping-ground for his army on the grassy plain, until Judith chopped off his head.

Daoud followed an indistinct trail directly across the plain. But it must have been the wrong one, for we were soon in the midst of a swamp. Daoud got very much excited when his ass struck a soft place and sank deep into the ooze. I somewhat enjoyed his excitement, for which there was no great cause. There were several hoof-marks of cattle leading through the soft places in different directions. Besides he allowed his ass to go so slowly that it could not but sink into the ooze. On no account would he allow me to proceed until he should have crossed. He called a boy, who was at some distance herding cattle, to show him the way. But he was afraid to follow the direction the boy gave. Seeing that he made no headway, I spurred my horse into a run, and followed the old tracks I had seen leading into the morass. My horse floundered through the insidious ooze, sinking deeper and deeper, while Daoud still stood at the edge shouting his lamentations and warnings after me. With a little scare I got safely to the other side. Daoud would not follow, and made a wide detour, where he at last scrambled through with his mule.

We again briskly pursued our way across the plain. Several large, beautiful black and white birds permitted us to approach within a few yards before they took flight. A flock of ducks also flew across the plain.

It seems poor Daoud's nerves were altogether unstrung by his adventure in the swamp, for he was now continually grumbling and prodding his ass. He turned around very often, making impatient signs for me to hasten, though I did not lag behind. The foothills were soon reached and we entered through wheat patches into an ascending ravine. The sun had disappeared, and the anxiety of Daoud probably arose from the fear of not being able to reach Sedabdieh, whither the priest in Naplouse had directed him for the night. The road was again exceedingly rugged, and dusk had begun to settle before we reached the top of the ravine. Daoud pushed aside some of the shrubbery, and gave a grunt of satisfaction when he saw the village lying in the valley below. He hastened down into the valley with his ass, and led the way between some ruined passages to a church on one side of the village. The penetrating smell of burning dung filled the air. The priest was not at home, but he arrived shortly after in company with an Arab priest, who had come on a visit. When Daoud told him that he had brought another priest as a guest for the night, he turned to me and asked me in Arabic, where the visitor was. I answered in French, that I was fearfully tired and hungry, and longed for some rest. Still more puzzled, he repeated his question, for he took me for an Arabian dragoman. It was only after a good deal of explanation, that he became used to the idea that I was his visitor, and a priest in a sheik's outfit. When once he understood the real situation he was hospitality itself.

Now that I had a prospect of obtaining some rest, a feeling of complete exhaustion overtook me. I had no desire for anything but sleep and rest. How glad I was when the father showed me a room where I could lie down! I fell at once into a sound sleep, and the kind priest must have had a great time to wake me two hours afterwards for supper. He had put himself, no doubt, to some trouble to procure some extra dishes, but I could hardly keep my eyes open while partaking of them. The priests in these countries must be extremely poor, and they no doubt live on almost nothing. Though the two priests seemed anxious to have a talk with me after dinner, I begged them to allow me to go to sleep. The resident priest seemed to be a Frenchman, while his other guest was a full-blooded Arab, who could speak only Arabic. He was on the way to Nazareth, his native town. The long sleep completely restored me, and I awoke in the morning ready to resume my journey.

Daoud waited with impatience until I finished mass in the little mission chapel and partook of a breakfast. My host would not accept payment for his hospitality, so nothing was left to do but to leave it in the form of stipends. The sun was already far up in its diurnal span when Daoud, the Arab priest, and myself were crossing the valley to Djenine, on the other side of some distant hills. The priest wore a cassock, and over his head a white tarbush, which fluttered in the wind as he rode along. He was mounted on a fine horse and usually took the lead on the trail.

At about eleven o'clock we came to Djenine, the scriptural Engannin, where Jesus healed the ten lepers. An abundant fountain gushes out of the hillside, which runs by the few miserable dwellings of Djenine and crosses the great plain of Esdrelon, which now spread out before us. On the spot where Jesus met the lepers a large Greek or Russian convent is built, but the inmates are so fanatic that my companions would not consent to visit it. From the gardens of this convent, in which are planted a great many fig and olive trees, an old aqueduct is built, and crosses the trail over an arch. It formerly carried the waters of the Kison over the surrounding higher lands for irrigation. Now, however, the clear waters rush out of the gardens through a break in the aqueduct, forming a limpid stream across the trail and through the sloping plain of Esdrelon. The sight of this brook, gushing from beneath the shade of luxurious trees, is extremely refreshing to the dusty traveler in Palestine, as he comes from the barren and rocky mountains of Judea.

The plain of Esdrelon is one of the most extended and beautiful in Palestine. To the right or east, little Hermon, and farther on, Tabor rise as landmarks; to the left, Carmel shuts out the view to the sea. In the mountains of Gilboe, which flank to the right, Saul met his defeat and death. The Kison flows through the midst of the plain. Some parts of the plain are dotted with wheatfields, whereas the middle portions of it afford fine pasture for the cattle. The roads, or paths rather, are free from rocks and it was a pleasure to traverse them. About half way across the plain gadflies began to swarm around my horse and he became quite unmanageable. Daoud began to shout at me "de bain," "de bain," as if in danger of death, and made the horse still more frenzied. As I did not know what he meant, I dismounted and let Daoud take charge of him, while I got on the ass. As long as these asses of Palestine choose to keep agoing they are very pleasant and easy to ride. But woe to the traveler when they get tired out, he will have to expect a thousand vexatious tricks. Daoud, after vainly trying to quiet the horse, soon again preferred the ass.

Nain was visible to the right. It is the village where Jesus called the son of the widow back to life, as they were carrying him out of the city gates for burial. There are no walls or gates at Nain now, only a collection of ruins, which give shelter to the few poverty-stricken inhabitants. Not far from Nain, at the foot of Mount Hermon, are the caves of Endor, where Saul persuaded the witch to conjure up the prophet Samuel. Instead of receiving the assurance of victory over his enemies, he heard the judgment of God pronounced against him. That day he came to an ignominious end. Mount Tabor, which had been hidden from sight by the mountains of Gilhoe, became visible as we approached the farther limits of the plain of Esdrelon. Nazareth lay in a hollow on the rocky heights of Galilee ahead of us. As we began to climb the rough trail we passed a group of armed Arabs, who scanned us with sinister looks. Farther up a few more seemed to stand as scouts. As our appearance was not particularly promising, we were not molested.

NAZARETH

CHAPTER IX.

NAZARETH AND ITS SANCTUARIES — BROTHER JEAN
— INFESTED REGIONS — ENCOUNTER ON NOTED
GROUNDS — BLIGHTED SHORES OF GALILEE — AN
ARAB WEDDING AT NIGHT — IN THE HANDS OF A
BOATLOAD OF FANATIC MOSLEMS.

Nazareth is not visible from the plain, for it is hidden
on a high plateau. It is a friendly-looking town, like
Bethlehem. People seem to be more prosperous and
the country around is better cultivated. Trees peer
over the houses and there are orchards on its outskirts.
Just as we reached the fine wagon road that was built
from Haipha to Nazareth in the expectation of the German emperor's visit, two kawasses came galloping past
on white horses in advance of a carriage just coming
from Haipha. These kawasses like to show their horsemanship and look quite gallant when they approach
a town where they know there is no need of using their
arms. But I suspect they are not so frisky when they
come into the presence of the roving Bedouins. No
doubt they would afford small protection in an attack.

Daoud brought us directly to the Franciscan hospice
in Nazareth. These hospices are useful institutions in
Palestine, for there the pilgrim finds welcome shelter at
all times. The poor are received with as much hospitality as the rich. The fees are very moderate, and
if any one should not be able to pay, he will no doubt
be allowed to depart in peace. The Franciscans are
found established at most of the holy places, and it is
only of late that other Catholic orders have opened
hospices in Jerusalem also. But it seems that at the

73

Nazareth hospice the line is drawn at an Arab sheik. They would not believe that I was a Christian pilgrim, much less a priest. Fortunately for me, Bishop Kelly from Australia just happened to meet me in the reception room. As I had spoken to him in Casa Nova at Jerusalem, he recognized me in spite of the Bedouin clothes. Then brother Jean, highly amused at my enterprise, received me quite cordially and assigned a room for my use. During his long experience he had not met a pilgrim who made use of such a scheme to evade the marauding Arabs. Daoud, after receiving the stipulated pay, returned to Naplouse that afternoon.

After sending a despatch to my companion in Jerusalem, Brother Jean personally conducted me and Rev. Westermeyer, a priest from Tucson, Arizona, to the noteworthy places in Nazareth. In the upper part of the town is the Mensa Christi. It is a large stone about three feet high and six by nine square, with an almost flat surface on top, where Christ is said to have eaten with his apostles after the resurrection. A fine chapel is built over this stone. Farther down, in one of the crooked streets, are the remains of the synagogue, whence the enraged Jews dragged Jesus in order to precipitate him from the cliff. This latter is about a half mile out of town, in a rugged defile in the mountain. The most remarkable place in Nazareth will always be the place where the Blessed Virgin lived and where the angel appeared unto Mary to announce the miraculous conception of the Son of God. This spot is behind the hospice, inside of a beautiful church. It is built up on the old foundation of St. Helen's church, covering the former site of the holy house of Loretto, and the caves, that formed part of the dwelling of Jesus, Mary and Joseph.

As you enter the church you see a magnificent high altar rising above the platform in front. This platform is about fifteen feet higher than the main body of the church and forms the sanctuary. The church is beautifully decorated throughout and the stained glass windows shed through it a mellow light. Under the platform are the crypts or caves, which were a part of the dwelling of the holy family. Fifteen marble steps, about twelve feet wide, lead down to the first cave. On the spot where Mary knelt as She received the message of the angel and where She gave her blessed consent to the Incarnation, stands the altar of the Annunciation. Lights are continually burning in front of it. The walls of the cave are covered with marble slabs, with the exception of the pillar to the left, where the angel hovered, when he brought the message. What Christian's heart is not moved in places like this, where such heavenly mysteries transpired? Here heaven came in contact with the earth; here the darkness of sin was dispelled by the light of heaven; here God asked the lowly Virgin to become his Mother.

Behind the altar is another cave, which is said to have been the kitchen of the holy family. Adjoining this, a third cave formed another apartment. The brother showed us certain remnants which indicated in what position the house of Loretto must have stood and how it was joined to the caves so as to form one dwelling with them. It was, and is even now, very common among the Jews to build their dwelling over the openings of caves in such a way so as to make use of them as part of the abode. The miraculous transportation of the holy house of Loretto is such a well authenticated fact that none but the hypercritical find difficulty in believing it. As I knew that it would not be very long before I would see Loretto, I took particular notice of circumstances relating to this sacred spot and the sanctuary of Loretto. Any one that weighs well the evidences will come to the conclusion that such a house as that at Loretto has once stood here.

The workshop of St. Joseph is not far from the church of the Annunciation; here the Crusaders had built a large basilica, of which only the foundations remain. They have been excavated by the Franciscans and are plainly visible. A chapel occupies that part of the foundations which enclose the old workshop. They have also succeeded in buying up all the space intervening between the church and the workshop, with the exception of a small lot, so that very soon all the space connected with the workshop of her spouse and the dwelling place of the holy family will be under Franciscan custody.

The next morning I said holy Mass on the spot where the blessed Virgin received the message from the angel, and where the word was made flesh. In the credo of every Mass said on this altar the priest says, "Hic verbum caro factum est," i. e., "Here the word was made flesh." Brother Jean is quite an original character and well fitted for the office he holds as manager of the hospice. He speaks seven different languages. The French priests fare badly in his estimation. Out of hundreds of them that he had met, only two of them acknowledged that the French people are falling away from the faith. Those two, however, had told him with tears in their eyes, that religion has no hold on the men in France and that the churches are filled mostly by the women. If it is necessary to see an evil before it can be corrected, then this wilful blindness of the French clergy is certainly a bad omen. Three American priests were camping at the foot of the hill on the outskirts of Nazareth. They were in charge of a dragoman and were paying 850 francs apiece for his services as guide. This is an enormous price. My expenses had not yet amounted to 30 francs, and Rev. Westermeyer, who traveled alone with a moukar, will make the journey from Jerusalem to Nazareth, Tiberias, Tabor, and Haipha for about 140 francs. Of course he must stop over night wherever he finds accommodation, like myself. One that does not know how to be independent of dragomen is at their mercy. They increase their demands in proportion as one is dependent upon them.

After dinner brother Jean sent me a moukar, who was to bring a horse for my trip to Tiberias and return. The moukar brought a horse furnished with Arab saddle and stirrups. But the wily moukar, instead of accompanying me to take care of the horse, as was agreed, at the first turning of the road, left me and the horse in charge of a battered and ragged piece of humanity, who was partly lame, almost blind, and not altogether too sharp of hearing. I did not much care or take notice of him at first, but when I perceived that in addition he was not very sure of the way, all his other deficiencies became so much the more annoying. Just as we were leaving Nazareth, an Arab woman ran past us with dishevelled hair and screaming. She was pursued by a furious Arab, who soon seized her by the hair and struck her in the face. The maddened woman seized a large stone to hurl it at the man. I suppose this is one of the amenities of married life in the Arab harems.

On the outskirts of the town we passed the fountain of Mary, which is the only source of fresh water for Nazareth. Two large jets gush from a ruined alcove into a trough and from there meander down the valley. All day long the women of Nazareth are seen gathered around this fountain, filling their earthen jars, washing their clothes and, womanlike, gossiping with each other. Dexterously they balance the large jars containing three or four gallons of water on top of their heads and walk along the rough streets without spilling a drop. This accounts for the straight and upright carriage of their bodies, which is so noticeable in the women of Oriental countries. In the large families one of the females is deputed to do this water-carrying, and it keeps her busy most of the time. The water-jars in the Orient would do good service in running opposition to the ice companies in our own country. For the water exudes like perspiration through the porous earthenware; if the jar is then exposed to a current of air, the rapid evaporation of the thin moisture on the outside will keep the water cool and fresh. Travelers on horseback or on foot generally carry a small jar, in which the water is always kept in good condition by this process.

We left behind us several hills and passed a village before we came to Kep Kana, where Jesus changed the water into wine at the marriage feast. The Franciscans have erected a chapel over the foundations of an older church on the spot, where this first public miracle was wrought by the Savior. The guardian of the convent on Mount Tabor happened to be there on a visit. He invited me to the dwelling and regaled me with a glass of wine. A little farther on is another chapel on the site of Nathanael's house. About two miles from Kana, in a valley to the left, is seen the field, where the apostles, being hungry, plucked some ears of corn on the Sabbath. The Pharisees accused them of having thereby violated the sabbath, but Jesus defended them against their hateful aspersions. A fine field of grain was waving even then in the same spot. The meadows and fields hereabouts are in a pleasant contrast with the barren mountains of Judea and eastern Samaria, which I had traversed on the first two days. The road gradually ascends to a high ridge, about a mile to the left of the rude village Loubieh. The Kouroun Hattine, or hill of beatitudes, stands out boldly against the blue sky. Here Jesus is said to have taught the eight beatitudes, which have become the foundation of all Christian civilization. Six hundred years ago, the crusaders made their last stand against the Moslems under Saladin, but met great slaughter and defeat. It put an end to the kingdom of Jerusalem after a duration of less than one hundred years.

I desired to visit the summit of this mountain, where the beatitudes were first proclaimed, and I accordingly turned my horse off the road to ascend to its summit. But my moukar raised loud objections, calling out with violent gesticulations: "Harami, harami!" (robbers, robbers), refusing to follow. As the ground became too rough and broken, I dismounted and tied the horse to a projecting rock, motioning him to come and take charge of it, while I proceeded to climb the hill alone. The place looked lonesome and rugged enough, but as I did not see any sign of human life either around its sides or on its summit, I pushed on till I reached the plateau of the mountain. Ruins of an old church are still scattered about, while several rocks jut out around the edges, which give this mountain its present name of Kouroun, or Horns of Hattine. A beautiful view is had from this summit. To the northeast, at about seven miles distance, the large town of Saphet lies scattered over the brow of a hill. To the east, in a deep basin, surrounded by mountains, gleam the blue waters of Genesareth. Across the lake over the mountains of Moab, the snow-covered summit of the greater Hermon caught the rays of the evening sun. To the southeast stretches the woody valley of the Jordan, and in the southwest, Tabor's oval heights rise over the plains of Esdrelon. Carmel, behind it, shuts off the view of the Mediterranean Sea. The mountains of Galilee gradually merge into the higher Libanon range of Syria.

My spurt up the Mount of Beatitudes had consumed more time than I had calculated and the sun was now sinking. As I again resumed the saddle to traverse the broken ground back to our trail, a band of Bedouins were coming from an opposite direction along the road which I sought to regain. Two of them, on horseback and armed with carabines, halted as they saw us at a distance, and then left the road and crossed the fields in a gallop toward us. I did not know what their intention was, but it was evidently necessary to make some kind of a bluff, if I did not want to be molested. So I boldly changed my direction in order to meet them squarely. They halted within a dozen yards, grasping their guns. As a counter move I put my right hand to my belt as if ready to draw a weapon. Evidently they were puzzled and expected a parley at least. But they were bound to be disappointed. I said nothing, not even "Salaam," for my dignity of sheik, wearing a ten times better haik than they, required that they should greet me first. In a puzzled way they muttered that word of greeting as I rode closely past them. I answered with a surly "Aleikun." They must have readily understood, that I was not inclined to waste too much of my Arabic on them. But they detained my sorry guide and plied him with questions, while I rode on toward the trail. I don't know what fibs the guide told them about me, but they released him after a short parley and he came trudging on behind.

The path now descended rapidly down the bluffs to the basin of the lake. The dusk began to settle rapidly, and as it became quite dark, I took a side trail in the hope of reaching the valley sooner. The guide had completely lost his way and stumbled on behind me. I could do nothing but trust entirely to the instinct of my horse to bring me again to the main road. On either side, some distance from our course, Bedouins were heard, and groups of them were coming toward us, holding rude lanterns in our directions. I urged on my stumbling horse, loudly repeating the Arabic words which I had heard Daoud use in urging on his beasts of burden. In the dark of course the Arabs must have taken us for one of their own marauders returning to Tiberias.

Happily my horse again found the main road and long before we reached Tiberias, we saw tiny lights far down in the valley gleaming through the darkness. Coming nearer, we were surprised to find that the lights we had seen, were small bonfires and lanterns used by bands of Arabs outside the old city walls. They were celebrating some Mahomedan feast, and the dull rattling of drums and the sound of fifes supplemented the bonfires. The hospice of the Franciscans is built on the site of St. Peter's house. We had to grope our way through the garbage and half-ruined walls of several streets, before we came to its gate. Spanish fathers and two Brazilian brothers received me with laughing surprise at my strange garb. It was hard to do justice to their curious inquiries and to the substantial supper at one and the same time.

Afterwards one of the brothers conducted me to the flat roof of the three-storied hospice, in order to see something of an Arab wedding going on in one of the neighboring houses. Sounds of festive music and gaiety were heard long before the real ceremony took place. At about nine o'clock a crowd of young people and some men were seen coming slowly from the upper part of the town with lanterns and torches. In their midst the bride, entirely veiled, was led by some of her relatives over the rough street. The motley crowd of Arabs, young and old, kept up a continual singing and shouting, clapping of hands, and beating of cymbals. One shrill cry, like the long-drawn triller of frogs in early spring, sounded above all the rest of the noise. The flickering light of the torches lighted up the earnest faces of the swarthy crowd as they passed in front of the hospice. The bride disappeared behind the doors of the house, while most of the men and children remained outside in the courtyard and the street. Only the shrill frog-cry yet resounded at intervals from the interior of the house.

Half an hour later the clamor of a still larger procession was heard coming from a different direction of the city. It was the bridegroom seeking his bride. He was conducted down the same street by the light of flaring torches. A crowd of men were singing a monotonous song with alternate responses like a litany. They were moving along sideways in two rows, and at each response they bowed toward the bridegroom almost to the ground. Others waved their torches, struck the cymbals, or played the flutes. The bridegroom, blindfolded, and with hands loosely tied in front, was conducted by two guides through the narrow streets. The noise became louder as they passed the hospice, and ended in confused shouts as they arrived at the locked gates of the aforementioned courtyard. The whole procession seemed to be in suspense for a while, as the loud knocks at the gate resounded through the night. Now and then also the high, quavering notes of the frog-cry sounded from the interior of the house. At length the gate seemed to have been forced open, and the bridegroom, freed from his bonds, rushed alone into the yard, while the bride was seen rushing down a stairs. The whole scene was lit up fantastically by the flickering torches. They fell into each other's arms and disappeared together in one of the side doors to indulge their nuptial rites in sacred privacy. The whole crew of Arabs outside raised a shout, for, as in the regulation novel, the loving pair had found each other and were now united. There was nothing left for us but to descend from the roof of our hospice; the show was over.

The next day being the feast of Saint George, which is a duplex here (I mention this for the benefit of my clerical friends who are accustomed to celebrate it as a semi-duplex in the United States), I celebrated his mass in preference to that of St. Peter, which can be said every day of the year on this altar. After mass I hired a boat to row to the ruins of Magdala, Capharnaum, and Bethsaida. A lazier crew than the one I had happened on never pulled oars. Six had entered the boat besides the owner and myself. But only two of them at a time did any rowing. The rest of them lay dozing or chatting on the seats. Once or twice they were stung to exertion by the ridicule which I served out to them. Magdala is now a field of ruins, where bandits watch for unprotected travelers, or the jackal prowls about. The same may be said of Bethsaida and Capharnaum, only the ruins are more extensive. And yet the lands around seem to be more fertile than other parts of the country. The malediction of Jesus Christ over these once flourishing cities, as over the rest of Palestine, is literally fulfilled. For nearly all the towns and villages, even a great part of Jerusalem, are only heaps of ruins and the inhabitants are but the dregs of the many surrounding and distant nations, that have been left behind by the invading armies. I proposed taking a bath in mid-lake. But my swarthy boatmates would not hear of it, as a traveler had been drowned some time ago while out on the lake, and the crew of his boat had been seized under suspicion of having thrown him overboard. I believe it was just as well that they did refuse, for one or two of them had listened to some of my remarks about Mahomet with quite an angry scowl.

Lake Genesareth is a beautiful sheet of water some six miles wide by about ten long. The Jordan enters it from the north and issues again from thè south, flowing on about seventy miles to be lost in the salty waters of the Dead Sea. The mountains of Moab rise in high barren cliffs on its eastern shore. Only one of the many towns and villages that dotted its shores during the time of Christ still remains, Tiberias, containing about four thousand inhabitants. It is nothing but a large collection of ruins and mud-huts surrounded by crumbling fortification walls. The best building in Tiberias is the Franciscan hospice.

CHAPTER X.

Across Hill and Dale to Tabor's Heights — Surprising a Caravan — Sacred Shrines of Old — Again at Nazareth — Coaching to Haipha.

After dinner my worthy guide stumbled on ahead of me through a breach of the city walls, and up the high bluffs over a trail, which he guessed would bring us to Mount Tabor. On the top of the steep declivities, however, the trail branched out into several others going in different directions. As he blundered into a path, which led into the valley of the Jordan south of us, I simply recalled him and led the way across a spacious valley, which lay to the west, and at the head of which the horned crags of the Mount of Beatitudes lay northward. As I urged on my horse at a fast gait, he dropped behind, and had lost sight of me by the time my horse began to climb toward a ravine on the opposite ridge of hills. Like many others of the natives of Palestine, he suffered from sore eyes and was almost blind. The disease is brought on by handling dried figs, which contain a subtle poison. As they do not wash their hands very frequently, it is readily brought into contact with the eyes. When I was on the point of entering the ravine, I saw my guide far down in the valley, anxiously looking for me, and uttering doleful cries, though I was in plain sight. After waiting in vain for a while, I had to ride within a few yards of him before he saw me and heard my loud calls.

I pointed in the direction of Tabor and proceeded up the broken ravine. We were expecting to find a cool drink at the fountain head of a rippling stream, which purled down over the rocks, but our hopes vanished, when we saw several men and children bathing in the very trough of the spring. On the summit of the mountain is perched a half-ruined village, inhabited by bandit-like Arabs. From there we could distinguish the trail down the gradual descent to the foot of Tabor. About two miles farther on, Koud-el-khan guards the trail on both sides like two forts. It was formerly used as a gathering place for the cattle and camel drivers from across the Jordan and from the south. Here they made their exchange between Egypt and Arabia before the time of railroads and canals. Koud-el-khan is in ruins now and a favorite resort of nomad Bedouins. The neighborhood affords fine pastures and the small stream in the valley is fringed with growths of trees and shrub. Down on the other side of the stream, a tall Arab had dismounted from his white horse and was performing his prayers toward Mecca with many a profound bow and prostration. The mellow light of the evening sun fell across his gaunt, dark features. He took no notice of us as we forded the stream near by.

The country around Tabor is well wooded; the mountain itself is clothed in green, though the trees are not of large size. Shadows were now darkening the valleys, and the sinking sun slanted across our path, that zigzagged up among the trees and shrubbery of the western side of the mountain. But darkness had settled over the country before we arrived at the old fortification walls on the summit. The Franciscan hospice is on the eastern end of the oval-shaped plateau. The crusaders had built walls around the whole top; and a church on the ruins of an older one, which marked the spot of the Transfiguration. All these are now in ruins, near the hospice.

We were not a little surprised to find a cavalcade of horses tied up on the sides of the road. But that was soon explained when we came to the open door of a hall, from which lights were gleaming. In the hall a long table was set with many plates. About twenty members of the Cologne pilgrimage were standing or sitting, some of them in lively conversations. Father Custos, whom I had seen the day before at Kana, was standing opposite the entrance, talking to two of the caravan. He saw me enter, but thinking it was only one of the moukars of the caravan, took no further notice of me. I had to approach and assure him that I was the person he had seen yesterday. Then one of the caravan, by the name of Ruf, from Bavaria, came up and exclaimed: "O, das ist ja der Amerikaner!" Of course the rest of the party, with most of whom I had made the trip to Emmaus, now crowded up and fully identified me. I was busy answering their questions for the next hour during supper. I thought most of them looked pretty well worn out by their trip. One of them had his arm in a sling, as he had sprained it by a fall from his horse. All went to sleep early, for they wanted to continue on their way to Tiberias before sunrise in the morning.

At four o'clock sleep was cut short by the bustle and noise of preparation for their departure. I myself said mass in the chapel of the Transfiguration later on, and Father Custos showed me around after the caravan had left. The plateau of Tabor was first encircled by a wall under the Romans by Flavius Josephus, the historian. Later on the crusaders extended and strengthened these walls. When the Moslems again took possession of Palestine, they tore down the church and made great additions to the citadel in conformity with Oriental taste. The ruins of this citadel still cover a large area of the east end of the mount. To judge by these ruins there must have been a strong garrison and the commanders must have lived in magnificently furnished quarters. On the north side of the plateau the Russian monks have their own large establishment. Descending Tabor by the same trail on which we had come up, we took a road branching off to the left at the foot of the mount. We soon passed the village of Tabourieh and crossed a torrent. After surmounting three barren mountains on the farther side of the torrent, we pursued our way back to Nazareth. I was so tired out that I fell asleep on my stumbling nag several times. I had made the trip to Tiberias and Tabor in about half the usual time. The remaining part of the day was devoted to rest and sleep.

The next day there was quite a change in my mode of traveling. Father Hermann Schwarzer, of St. Peter's Institute in Jerusalem, was about to depart for Haipha in a carriage. I made arrangements to go with him. A native merchant was also in our company. We enjoyed the ride thoroughly, and I incidentally learned a little Arabic. He invited me to make a trip in a boat on the Jordan from Tiberias to the Dead sea. Of course I regretted very much that I could not spare the time. The scenery along the road is not so bad for a country like Palestine. Coming out of Nazareth over the brow of the hills and skirting along the mountains that border the plains of Esdrelon, we had some fine glimpses of Carmel and the Mediterranean. Reaching the plain we stopped at a picturesque khan, where an old Greek papa was sitting on a stool. He immediately asked me for some stipends. A few miles east of Haipha the road crosses the Kison. Along its valley a railroad is in course of construction for the last seven or eight years. They have already built four or five miles of road, and perhaps in fifty or sixty years they will reach Tiberias, that is, if they keep up the present rapid construction. But who can tell? There were at least a half dozen men at work on the road as we passed.

Haipha is a lively town, full of business, though on a small scale. It is built·on the north side of the long-stretched Carmel. But it is fully two miles distant from the end of the promontory, which the mountain forms. The shores of the Mediterranean make quite a bend around the mountain, so that Haipha is squeezed in between the north side of Carmel and the seashore.

Father Schwarzer betook himself to the convent of the Ratisbon German Sisters, while I intended to take lodging in the Franciscan hospice in Haipha. But the burly brother that opened the door eyed me suspiciously, and would have nothing to do with a Bedouin. Evidently he suspected that I came for no good intent, and he shut the door on me without ceremony. The next best thing to do was to try my luck at the door of the great Carmelite monastery, about a mile and a half up Mount Carmel. The sun was about to sink and its last rays fell upon the old buildings, which stood out in bold profile against the sky on the western bluffs of the mountain. The path leads gradually up the woody sides and passes round the front of the promontory. Again the French brother that received me was startled at my appearance, but I would not be put.off so easily this time: I simply stayed. Several times during the evening, as he sat opposite me and shaking his head, he said: "Pourquoi avez vous pris ces habiliments?" He could not understand why I did not travel in a cassock. To tell the truth, his scruples troubled me very little, as long as I had prospects of a good meal and a good sleep; they did not interfere with these.

CHAPTER XI.

WOODED CARMEL — STROLLS AT HAIPHA — FORCED
MARCHES ALONG MEDITERRANEAN SHORES — LODG-
ING IN A KHAN — LYDDA TO JERUSALEM ON THE
"LIMITED" — PRACTICAL HINTS.

On the next morning a German father showed me
the extensive buildings of the monastery and hospice.
The origin of this monastery dates back to the time of
Elias; for, ever since he dwelt in the cave over which
the church is built, hermits have sought retirement on
this isolated promontory. Many Essenes or Jewish
ascetics lived here before the coming of the Messiah.
After the ascension of Christ, Christians began to inhabit
the wild caves of the mountain. Since the twelfth century, Carmelite monks have located here. In the grotto
of Elias the most prominent object is the beautiful
statue of the Blessed Virgin above the high altar. From
the roof of the monastery there is an extensive view along
the shores of the Mediterranean to Akka and Beirout,
paralleled by the Libanus mountain-chain.

Brother Ambrose would not hear a word of my returning alone to Jerusalem along the seacoast. He
would not even give me any information regarding the
road, in order not to be accessory to any harm that
might befall me. He claimed that a lonely traveler
would certainly be held up by roving bands. As he was
so inflexible in his opinion, I decided to hunt up Father
Schwarzer in Haipha. At the convent where he was on
a visit, the sister would not unlock the iron picket gate
of the enclosure, when such a strange looking individual
as myself in Arab clothes desired entrance. But Rev.

Schwarzer soon set them at ease, and told them I was not quite as dangerous as I looked. He and the chaplain of the convent were just as emphatic in trying to dissuade me from going alone to Jerusalem by way of the plains of Samaria. But they finally yielded so far as to promise to procure a moukar with two horses. I was to set out early next morning.

In the afternoon, Father Schwarzer and I had quite an extended walk through the German Protestant Templars' settlement and up the long ridge of Mount Carmel. Everywhere along the slope of the mountain, the fields and vineyards of those thrifty colonists could be seen. Their houses, in the western part of Haipha, are surrounded by gardens, and look very neat. On the eastern end of Carmel they have an immense hospice in the midst of extensive vineyards. From here we could also enjoy a beautiful view of the plains of Esdrelon. The Kison, winding in many a graceful bend through the green valley, reflected the blue of the evening sky. Haipha lay at our feet far below, and the settlement of the Templars, with its rows of trees and the bright colored houses, contrasted pleasantly with the crumbling houses and shops of the Turkish settlement on its east end.

Next morning at sunrise, the moukar brought a fine horse, while he himself bestrode a mare, somewhat lame, but which kept up a lively pacing nearly the whole day. Like all Arabs, he was very monosyllabic, merely beckoning me not to lag behind. Our way led around the promontory of Carmel and then through the widening plains, which slope gently down the receding mountains to the sea. For the first ten or twelve miles the plains are pretty well cultivated, and our road was generally a mere path through the wheatfields. Our horses every now and then could not be restrained from cropping some of the ears at the side of the path, nor was my moukar so very anxious to restrain them. The way diverged from the seashore, so that at noon time, when we held our frugal meal in an immense vineyard, we were quite a distance eastward from Caesarea, which lies halfway between Haipha and Jaffa, on the shore of the Mediterranean. An hour later we came to a dilapidated water-mill by the side of a small stream. I wondered to find even that much enterprise, though the mill looked small and primitive enough. Some miles beyond this we crossed some marshy stretches, which again gave way to groupings of olive and other trees: a region quite different from the stony deserts of Judea and Samaria. My moukar pushed lustily onward, his limping mare always ahead and pacing most of the time. At about four o'clock, we had reached the plains of Samaria, where a gentle breeze from the sand dunes to the west softly swept through the ripening wheatfields around us. The soil must be very productive here and the people more industrious than in other parts of Palestine.

My moukar got into scarcely distinguishable by-paths and changed directions several times, evidently puzzled as to the right way. Ruinous villages were visible in the plains and on the hillsides, towards one of which we were tending at setting of the sun. I was in hopes it would prove to be the stopping place for the night, for we had been laboriously traveling since early morning. But the moukar hastened past a group of natives gathered at the well outside the walls, and pointed to a lonely building in a wide plain. At this khan we arrived at dusk and were received by a Turk in some kind of old uniform. The building consisted of four walls, enclosing a square courtyard, and so arranged as to form sheds for beasts toward the interior. Above one of these sheds one solitary small room was supposed to furnish shelter for travelers. I was not slow in dismounting and crossing the filthy courtyard to the sumptuous lodging upstairs. As I pushed open the door, three rude couches, a stool, and a rickety table gave but faint prospects of rest to tired limbs. But there was at least one of nature's best refreshments to be had: cool water. Immediately outside the door on the roof of the shed, a huge waterwheel was slowly revolving on its wooden axles driven by a mule downstairs. Creaking and groaning, it laboriously brought up small buckets full of water from the well and automatically emptied them into a trough. A stream of this water entered the room at one corner and flowed in an open gutter on the floor and out through an opening at the opposite end. Here it splattered down into a large stone reservoir outside the walls of the house to be distributed for irrigation through the adjoining fields. I thought it a fine arrangement and I immediately procured the luxury of a cool footbath in the running stream.

But I waited in vain for something to eat, and not until I had hunted up my moukar, did the keeper bring up a little of the pancake-bread, no better than that which I had refused to eat on the first two days of my trip. In addition, also some eggs, fried in dirty grease, and a tin-cup full of coffee. The moukar and myself partook of this frugal meal; that is, I tried to make my moukar eat it all, if possible, for I had not yet arrived at such a point of starvation as to relish the disgusting victuals. He was not at all slow to seize such an advantage. A third, most ragged inmate had entered and thrown himself on one of the couches, while the moukar and myself sought the others. However, I soon found out, that if these couches were not padded with blocks of wood, they must have been lined with harder and more uneven boulders. Music also was not wanting in this hostelry; besides the insidious songs of bloodthirsty gnats, my moukar and the other inmate vied in stentorious snores in all varieties of deepfelt expression, minuendos, crescendos, and fortissimos,—literally "to beat the band" of mosquitos. Many times during the night I turned on that merciless couch, where even weariness could not woo the blessed sleep.

Next morning we found ourselves again astride of our horses traversing the gentle undulations of Samaria. Early in the forenoon, a large caravan of camels heralded their approach from afar by their peculiar odor. The Arabs smear some kind of grease or tar over the skin of the camels in order to protect them from flies and from the exposure of travel. This, of course, does not add any particular attractiveness to a herd of these patient animals. Some miles farther, one of the camels had been left to its fate by the Arabs, probably because its days of service were at an end. About noon, Lydda, where I was to take the train for Jerusalem, hove into distant view. Miles and miles of the finest wheatfields lay yet between, and it seems that here the fruitfulness of the Holy Land is fully up to its old record. Around Lydda large olive orchards, fenced by high cactus hedges, lined both sides of the road. Lydda is but a collection of the usual ruinous huts, though in the first century it was the centre of an important diocese and, no doubt, a large town. St. George was born here, and for several centuries his body rested in a large and beautiful church. Now there is only a crumbling Greek chapel on the site of the former cathedral. The habitation of the Russian monks, who have charge of this spot, stands near by in no better condition.

The railroad station is about one mile from the village. I had just enough gold left to give the moukar two napoleons and pay the fare to Jerusalem. I was yet in time for an extra train, entirely empty, which on its return was to carry some hundreds of Russian pilgrims back to Jaffa. On the train I could stretch myself in full length upon the vacant benches, until we reached Jerusalem. At the hospice, the first one who welcomed me was Ali, and I learnt that my absence had caused some apprehension. My traveling companion had in the meanwhile suffered a severe attack of the fever peculiar to Jerusalem, and had been out of the house only twice during the ten days of my absence. He had many words of praise for the excellent care taken of him during his sickness. It seems he had also worried a great deal about my safety.

PRACTICAL HINTS. To a Christian traveler the Holy Land must always be the most interesting land on earth. For here our Salvation was begun, and here is, as it were, the focus of all the world's history and of civilization. But in order to arrive at a true estimate of the things seen in the Holy Land, it is absolutely necessary to be somewhat informed of the history of the Jews and of the Christian faith. Moreover, all must be viewed in the light of faith. Thousands of tourists depart after a few days' stay, entirely disgusted with the ruinous appearance of many remarkable spots, the warring and strife between different religions, the poverty and degradation of the inhabitants. Thus, instead of seeing their ideals of the holy places realized, they find them entirely destroyed. But let the traveler look beneath the surface and try to account for the conditions, and he will depart strengthened in faith and even much edified. In order to obtain such a result, it is necessary to make a longer stay. No visit to Palestine is complete without including the tour to Jericho, Bethlehem, and Nazareth, at least. Traveling in a caravan is expensive and soon irksome. It is better to incur a little more trouble and hardship, and make the trip with a moukar. Of course carrying tents is then out of the question. The company of one or two friends will make the trip still more pleasant. The expenses of a trip with a moukar are not high. The dangers of being robbed are probably much exaggerated by tourist agencies and dragomen, who would, of course, lose customers by the more venturesome mode of travel. I do not see what three or four healthy Europeans would need to fear from the roving Bedouins, even if there would be a band of them. Besides, if they dress in poor garb, they would be in no danger, even singly. Plunder is what attracts the Bedouin. He will not seek it, where none is evident.

CHAPTER XII.

Ecce Homo Arch — Saint Anne's Tomb — The Cave of the Agony — Russian Foresight — Among Old Tombs and Monuments — St. Peter's Institute — Caverns of Jerusalem.

After a short rest we were again on our tour of visits to notable places in and around Jerusalem. One of our first was to the church and convent of Ecce Homo. The arch of the Ecce Homo is said to be a remnant of the platform on which the perfidious Pilate exhibited the Savior in a red military cloak after the scourging, and the crowning with thorns. It is about thirty feet high and curves from the right side of the narrow street into the wall of the recently built chapel of the Ratisbon convent, which is only a short distance from our hospice along the street running straight to St. Stephen's gate. What a fearful sight it must have been for the few faithful souls, to see our Savior standing on the high porch, streaming with blood, his body only half covered by the loose mantle, and his very skull pierced by the long thorns of the horrid crown; and how the cry: "Crucify Him, crucify Him," from the infatuated populace must have resounded like echoes from deepest hell! How terribly the curse of his blood has descended upon the race and all their children! Throughout the world they are now scattered, without temple, without worship, without hope of return to the land of their forefathers. Against their will they are witnesses of the power of Him whom they then despised.

Some rods farther along the same street, amid heaps of ruins, are some very old tombs, which the Moslems hold in high veneration. This does not mean, however, that they lavish much care on the outward appearance of the tombs. They are allowed to fall to ruin no less than the crumbling walls around them. Going out of St. Stephen's gate and crossing the Kidron, one comes to a level piece of ground, paved with stone flags. One of the Franciscans told us, that no doubt most interesting remains will be found beneath them if once they can obtain possession and start excavations on the spot. On one side of this level plat rises the front wall of one of the oldest churches in Jerusalem. It is the reputed tomb of the Virgin Mary. The body of the church is buried almost to the eaves beneath the accumulated debris. From the above mentioned court, a pavement leads down to a wide flight of marble stairs, descending about thirty feet to the original floor of the church. The church was formerly in charge of the Franciscans, but is now in the hands of the Russian monks and of the Armenians.

It is seldom opened for visitors, but profiting of such an occasion a few days later, we joined the crowds of pilgrims, that were attending service in honor of the Blessed Virgin. Half way down the stairs, in niches built off a break in the descent, are the tombs of St. Joachim and Anne to the right, and of St. Joseph to the left. The body of the church is entirely dark, for the debris outside rises higher than the windows. Only the open door above and the flickering light of the candles dispelled some of the darkness within. The church is built in the shape of a cross, formed by caves on three ends, and the stairs on the fourth. The drawling chant of the Armenian priests sounded up to us from the right arm of the church. Pressing through the crowd we saw the red-robed priests officiating before a monument or tomb. The light of candles shone from the openings of this tomb and lit up the faces of the bystanders. The priests had to stoop almost to the ground in order to enter through the small opening to the interior of the tomb. They were chanting alternate responses with the choir outside. While we wormed our way through the worshipers, there was a sudden commotion in front: two priests came out through the narrow opening of the tomb bearing two chalices to an altar in the background. One of them with a golden spoon, dealt out morsels steeped in some liquid to the people. They came up and stood before him with their hands dangling down their sides. I did not think their way of dealing out holy communion particularly reverend. The people began to squeeze into the narrow opening on the side of the tomb and file out at the other end; we among the rest.

The interior of the tomb presents nothing remarkable, except the brilliant illumination. Beneath a slab or table of marble, fitting into a recess, is said to be the last resting place of Mary. Here lay the sacred body of the Virgin and from this spot, reunited to her immaculate soul, it was assumed into heaven to be seated at the right hand of her son, as Queen of the universe. What a glorious sight it will be for us, if we shall once be privileged to see Her in her glory! That alone would be worth more than the possession and enjoyment of all the rest of the created things. To the left of the stairs is a well, the waters of which are held sacred. This church dates back to the time of Constantine and was always in possession of the Latins; but by the united rapacity of the Russians, Armenians, and Copts, the Franciscans have been deprived of its custody. Confusion and neglect surround the tomb of the Virgin in consequence. The vault of the whole interior is black with soot and dirt and no attempt is made to decorate in a befitting manner so sacred a place.

On the same morning I said Mass in the grotto of the Agony, which is only fifty steps or so from the tomb of Mary. It is a very large cave of oval shape. In the rear stands the altar, where colored lights are maintained day and night by the Franciscan brother, who is in charge. On the rough rocks above are still seen the remains of ancient paintings. Under this dark roof, prostrate on the hard rocks, Jesus began his passion. Three times He interrupted his prayers in order to console his apostles, who were lying under the olive trees outside. While we were there several Russian pilgrims came in. The principal part of their devotion seems to consist in making the sign of the cross and kissing the ground or any object which happens to strike their fancy. They make the sign of the cross from right to left. Shaggy these men and women look, with their heavy top boots and coarse clothing. They are harmless in their simplicity and full of happiness in being privileged to see the holy places. The paternal Russian government pays most of the expenses of their journey, well knowing that they are but forerunners of the hundred thousands, that will rise to wrest Palestine from the hands of the Turks. No doubt these Russian peasants return to their native provinces as missionaries for a holy war of conquest against the Turk.

The garden of Gethsemane is only some hundred yards from this grotto, nearer to the torrent of Kidron. The little postern gate, which we had found locked on Holy Thursday night, was now opened as we knocked. A gravel walk leads around along the quadrangular walls and the centre of the garden is enclosed by a picket fence. Stations of the cross are placed in niches of the outer wall and inside the picket fence some flowerbeds filled out the space between the knarled olive trees. The olive trees look old enough to have been standing at the time of Christ, though this is not ascertainable. A Franciscan brother lives in a cell near the hothouse. He entertained us with a glass of wine and gave us some flowers for preservation.

From the garden we wound our way up the rain-worn path to the top of Mount Olivet. It is the highest mountain around Jerusalem and the summit is an almost oval plateau a half mile long. The Russians own pretty well the whole summit of Olivet, with the exception of a cluster of ruinous Arab houses on the slope towards Jerusalem. On the western end extensive walls enclose a large garden and convent of Russians, and on the eastern end stands the church of the Ascension, flanked by a bell tower, which is very likely intended to serve as a Russian observation tower in time of war. In the church, Russian popes are chanting some kind of service with their customary frequent use of incense. The church is octagonal in form and most beautifully frescoed. In spite of the high wind that was blowing, I desired to climb the tower, which is about 30 feet square all the way up and nearly 200 feet high. Ostensibly, it seems to have been built for no other purpose than to support a chime of bells. But as it stands on the highest part of the country, it will serve as an observation tower for the whole region.

From its top one has a vast view of the surrounding country. To the west the Holy City lies spread out, the bare spot of the ancient temple grounds contrasting with the confused jumble of ruinous houses of the city. Beyond the further wall, the Russian settlement stands out prominently, with the great hospice and the convents as a centre. On clear days Ramleh and Jaffa, on the edge of the blue Mediterranean, can be seen. To the left and behind the plains of Jericho, the dead sea, and farther north, Moab and Harmon gleamed in the sunlight. To the northeast, Carmel and Libanus girt the plain of Esdrelon. As I descended the wind almost carried me out of the high gothic windows, which are left entirely open. The interior construction of the tower is of iron, and the outside shows uncommon architectural beauty.

From the tower we passed through the village to the place whence the Savior ascended into heaven. It lies a little lower down the hill and is covered by an octagonal mosque inside of an enclosure. The Franciscans are allowed to hold services within the enclosure once a year on Ascension day. The mosque is small and neglected, entirely bare. The ragged keeper showed us a stone in the center, imbedded in the ground, or more likely forming part of the natural rock. On this stone were the impressions of two feet, which are said to have been left by Christ as he ascended into heaven. I found, however, very little resemblance of footprints in the indentures; perhaps the marks have become disfigured in the course of centuries or through the vandalism of pilgrims. There is nothing unreasonable or improbable in the assertion, that such marks have been left by the Savior and by holy men on particular occasions, though sometimes superstition and the hope of gain will give rise to spurious fabrication of marks of the kind.

Descending on the road to the left, we passed the caves where St. Pelagia did penance for many years. Further on is the church of the Pater Noster and Credo, with the convent of the Carmelite nuns, where Jesus wept over the reprobate city. The Temple grounds are in full view and the city lies spread out beyond them. Beneath us, skirting the declivities of the city walls, gaped the valley of Josaphat, and merging into the valley of Hinom to the left. Far below on the banks of the Kidron rose Absalom's tomb. We descended to the brook and clambered up through the rugged cavities of the monument. It seems to have been cut out entirely from the native rock. The lower part is in the shape of a square kiosk, surmounted by a bottle-shaped top. It must be fully sixty feet high. No sort of care is taken of it, and the interior is full of crumbling stones. Aside of it is the tomb of St. James, also hewn out of the rock in the form of a small Greek temple. Ascending the other side of the Kidron, we came to the city walls, where some of the original stones of the temple of Solomon are still visible. Moslem graves cover nearly the whole declivity of the mountain along the city walls. Among these graves we stumbled, following the walls to St. Stephen's gate. At the hospice all was hustle and excitement to prepare for the arrival of 522 Austrian pilgrims from the diocese of Linz. The largest portion of these, with Bishop Doppelbauer at their head, were to lodge at our hospice.

In the afternoon our search for mail brought us again near the Jaffa gate. Mail service in the Turkish dominions is something very uncertain and therefore the Austrian, the English, and the German governments maintain separate post offices in Jerusalem, which insure some kind of safety, (though not any great expedition) to the mail from foreign countries. I had to wait three weeks after getting my letter of instruction, before I could obtain the payment of a money order in the Austrian post office.

I wished to visit Father Schwarzer, who by this time must have returned from Haipha. In order to reach St. Peter's institute for boys, of which he was in charge, we crossed the Mohammedan graveyards around the birket Mamilla, or tank of Solomon. This is an immense square reservoir, hewn thirty feet into the solid rock. It is now dried out. In this neighborhood the angel of God struck down 185,000 of Sennacherib's besieging army. Beyond, on a gently sloping hill, lies St. Peter's Institute. The father was glad to see me and returned to me the articles and the money which I had given in his keeping at Haipha. The classes and workshops of the boys were closed, it being a holiday; but we saw the interior of the extensive buildings and admired the beauty of the chapel. This is one of the several grand institutions, which Ratisbonne founded after his miraculous conversion in Rome.

Diverting on our return toward the Damascus gate, we came upon the grand basilica of the Dominicans. It is reared on the foundations of an ancient church in honor of St. Stephen. Twenty feet of rubbish had to be cleared away in order to bring to the light of day the curious mosaics of the original floor. Parts of these are incorporated with the fine mosaics of the present pavement. In the middle of the basilica a crypt is restored, which probably once contained the relics of St. Stephen. A number of the doric pillars rest upon the original pedestals. This church is no doubt the finest and the most costly in Jerusalem.

Not far from this church are the remarkable excavations called the tombs of the kings. They are a regular city of the dead, carved thirty feet deep out of the solid rocks. A wide stairs led down to two different divisions. The first one is filled about half with water, the other compartment is honeycombed on one of its four sides with small cells, which formerly contained the sarcophagi of the kings. In some of them the sarcophagi are still standing, rifled however, of their contents. Thus the ashes of the kings, that tried to hide themselves away after death, have been scattered to the winds, while thousands of their more humble subjects are still resting in their graves undisturbed. Returning through the dusk, we were curious to know more of a fine church and parsonage, which we had noticed on the way out. Many well dressed Europeans had just come out of the building. We found out from the attendant, that it was the Protestant Episcopal church, and presided over by Bishop Cheney. He had just given confirmation to a number of young people. The interior was finely decorated, but there was nothing in it which could be venerated as sacred, as in Catholic churches.

The vast grotto of Jeremias is some hundreds of yards eastward of the Damascus gate. The Moslem in charge showed us the stone ledge, which Jeremias used at a couch. The large cavern in the side of the hill, at even ground with the entrance, is connected by a passage to the left with another cave underground, in which Jeremias was imprisoned. It is now filled with water: a stone thrown into it resounded with a hollow splash, which gloomily reverberated through the subterranean darkness.

When we came to the hospice the Austrian pilgrims had arrived. During their stay we were placed at the table opposite to the bishop, who is a very affable man. The Rev. Rector Czarski had assigned us a room next to his own, and we were scarcely inconvenienced by the great crowds that now filled every available space of the building. For the following morning we had made arrangements for our trip to Jericho and the Dead Sea.

CHAPTER XIII.

Surrounded by Lepers — A Howling Wilderness —
To the Dead Sea — A Plunge in the Jordan —
In the Clefts of Quarantania — Greek Hos-
pitality — Robbers' Inn and Bethany — With
the Austrian Pilgrims — In the Cenacle —
Unsaddled.

A burly Arab driver by the name of Mahomet had
charge of the carriage in which we made our trip to
Jericho. Noisily the wheels rattled over the cobbles to
St. Stephen's gate. A bevy of lepers were sitting and
lying in the bright sunshine along the road as we moved
down the hill to the Kidron bridge. We threw some of
them a few metaliques. No sooner had those farther
behind and ahead seen this, than a howl rose from their
midst. Those that were able to move surrounded the
carriage, stretching out their leprous hands, and some
of them even grasping hold of our garments in order to
obtain an equal share of the alms. Mahomet unceremoniously threatened them with his whip before he
could drive through their midst and escape. The
macadam road, built in honor of the German Emperor's
visit to Jericho, leads around the south side of Mount
Olivet to the ruins of Bethany, down the deep ravine
to the Apostles' fountain, and some six miles farther to
the government khan of the good Samaritan. It will be
more convenient to speak of them later on.

All this country from Bethany to the plains of Jericho
is a howling wilderness. No spring or any kind of
stream is found from the Apostles' well to the Nahr-el-
Kelt, about three miles beyond the khan of the good

Samaritan. The Nahr-el-Kelt is a ravine, eaten through the rocks by a small stream which takes its rise near the road. It is the most rugged ravine I had yet seen, surpassing even the wild gulches of the Wasatch mountains in Utah. Sheerly down through the broken granite rocks the slender stream leaps from ledge to ledge, having formed for itself a mere cleft through the mountains to the plains of Jericho. About a mile from where we stood, a monastery is built on the ledges of the ravine, three or four hundred feet above the bottom. The buildings were mere stone huts, leaning against the cliffs, and they seemed altogether inaccessible. They are tenanted by Russian monks.

A mile farther on brought us to the edge of the mountains. The road here makes a steep and dangerous descent to the plains of Jericho. In the ruined village of Jericho, there are three lodging-houses, all bitter rivals. Mahomet seemed to stand in with the young man who runs the Gilgal hotel, and we did not object to his bringing us there for our dinner and lodging. The slopes running up from the Dead sea and the Jordan are entirely barren, except where the ground is irrigated by the fountain of Elisha.

In the afternoon Mahomet drove helter skelter over these plains to the Dead sea, raising clouds of dust. The nearer we came to the sea, the more arid and dusty grew the roads and the country around. The Dead sea looks like any other lake from afar. The waters are grayish blue, and perfectly clear. On the farther side the mountains of Moab rise like a wall of bare rocks, while to the south only a blue ridge is dimly visible above the glittering waters. Being alone we took a bath. The water is so heavy that it is impossible to sink. Lying flat, half the body is always out of the water. But if the feet are raised, the head immediately sinks beneath the surface and the brine will enter the nose and mouth.

The skin is coated with salt in a short time; this causes a disagreeable sensation, unless it is washed off with fresh water. Just as we had partly dressed, another carriage came up with a Greek papa and a woman. Without much ado the papa undressed, leaving the woman in the carriage within a few steps of the shore. He made great ado in the shallow water before he plunged in to swim.

About three miles in a northeasterly direction is the place where the Israelites crossed the Jordan. Only scattered sage brushes are met with along the road before reaching the Jordan. There a species of tamarack and poplar forms thick bushes on the banks of the river. The river banks are very muddy. I sank into the mud to my knees, while bathing. The river is about forty yards wide, very deep, muddy, and swift running. Very often careless bathers meet their death in this place. Again the Greek papa came up with the lady, and stripped to take a plunge. Afterwards we hired a boatman to take us a little distance up the river. I was sorry not to be able to extend this boatride up to Lake Genesareth, and hoped I could do so on a future occasion. The short distance was exceedingly romantic. What a wall of water must have gathered to the north of this place, when the Jordan stood still, until the vast host of the Israelites had crossed, and how the waters must have rushed down again into the dry bed, when this was accomplished!

Driving home as the sun sank over the western hills, we met some shepherds and some reapers. The latter carried huge sheaves of grain home on their backs, reminding us of the words of the psalmist: "Venientes autem venient cum exultatione, portantes manipulas suos." We forded the Nahr-el-Kelt, which we had admired in the morning among the hills. In this neighborhood the Israelites encamped after crossing the Jordan, but nothing remains of Gilgal, and the memorial of twelve stones, which they set up. A large Russian convent, that of St. John, lies to the left at a few miles distance. Robbers infest these plains, for a young German, who stopped at our hotel, told me that he had two horses stolen from him on the plains of Jericho by marauding Arabs. Arriving at the hotel, we were surprised to see the Greek papa with his fair young lady sitting at table with us. Next morning before sunrise we drummed up the unwilling Mahomet to take us to Elisha's or Sultan's fountain, not far from Quarantine Mount. Its water runs close by Jericho and causes a streak of rich vegetation to spring up along its course. Flowering rhododendron lined the road in some places, and reminded us of balmy spring mornings of other countries. The abundant stream of pure water collects in a reservoir, from which it is branched off in different conduits to water the fields on the slopes. Ever since Eliseus changed its unwholesome water three thousand years ago, it has poured out refreshing streams over the arid plains of Jericho. The first rays of the sun rising over Moab, tinged the summit of Quarantania and the Greek convent leaning against the red rocks about midway up the declivities. The summit of this, the highest and most rugged of the Judean mountains, is now crowned by an irregular wall, enclosing the spot of the third temptation of Christ. In spite of the unwillingness of Mahomet to wait, we began our ascent. A stream traverses the foothills in the foreground, and in some valleys herds were grazing, and a few field laborers were already at work. Ruins of ancient Jericho are yet traceable on some of the foothills. At the foot of the mountain stands a house surrounded by gardens. It belongs to the monastery on the mount, and furnishes vegetables for the community. From here a very steep, zigzag trail leads up to the monastery, which seems literally suspended from the ledges of the rocks.

Panting from the exertion of the steep climb, we arrived at the rude door or gate and were admitted by the porter, who is on the watch for visitors. He treated us with arrack and a delicious cup of mocha. The narrow cells of the monks are mere cave abutments hewn into rocky walls of the mountain. A guide led us through narrow passages to the cave in which Jesus is said to have fasted for forty days. Beneath this cave is a larger one in which Elias lived for a while. It is almost inaccessible except by ladders or ropes. The long-haired Greek produced a ponderous key to open a gate, which gives access to the continuation of the path up to the summit. This has been enclosed recently by a stone wall; but there is nothing to mark the spot of the third temptation except a rude shed, and near it a large cross. The plains of Jericho and the valley of the Jordan lay now in full view beneath. Where the Jordan wound its way through the valley there is a streak of beautiful green, contrasting with the arid waste of the plain. The sun had risen high toward the zenith, and shot down burning rays as we climbed down again to reach the carriage.

We wanted to return to Jerusalem that day. Mabomet at first strenuously refused. The horses would not stand the exertion, he said. I suspect he merely wanted to play into the hands of the hotel-keeper by lengthening our stay. We had already resigned ourselves and were about to lie down for a siesta, when our offer of an extra bakshish had done its work. He now urged us to return to Jerusalem. His previous objections, however, were not all unfounded, for the mid-day heat, reflected from the rocks, almost overcame man and beast, as we climbed afoot up the first ascent to the Judean mountains. Mahomet made a stop of over an hour at the khan of the good Samaritan. This is an enclosure of about an acre for beasts of burden, with a rude shack for the accommodation of travelers. It is maintained by the government, but the only refreshment to be had in these khans is a cup of coffee. The country ten miles around is a howling wilderness of rocky mountains, an ideal place for such an incident as is related in the parable of the good Samaritan. On the hill behind the khan the ruins of an old fort can be seen.

We did not stop at the Apostles' inn, which is merely a small house inhabited by some enterprising native near a brackish fountain not far from Bethany. In this neighborhood the apostles are said to have often met after the Ascension of Christ. Bethany is scarcely two miles farther along the road, pretty well up on the east side of Mount Olivet. A ragged Arab is always on the lookout for strangers, to show them the tomb of Lazarus and the ruins of Lazarus' and Simon's house. He gave us some dirty candle stumps and preceded us down the series of caves, which form the tomb. Not the least sign of care or veneration is to be seen. Heaps of dirt and rubbish cover the stairs and the bottom of the caves. The tomb itself, from which Lazarus was called forth, is full of filth. We left disgusted, to have a look at the site of the two houses mentioned above. They are now covered with the ruins of chapels, probably built by the crusaders. Having reached St. Stephen's gate, Mabomet rattled in great style over the broken pavement to the hospice. When we alighted I found that I had lost my notebook on the way. Though I made every effort to recover it, I never saw it any more. However, as its contents covered only a short period of my journey, I replaced it pretty well with a synopsis from memory.

We were just in time to accompany the Austrian pilgrims on their visit to Mount Sion. Our first stop was made at the large Armenian convents and gardens, only a short distance beyond the tower of David. The fumes of incense filled the large church of St. James, which is built on the spot where he was decapitated. It is profusely decorated with tiles of different colors, and the altars and cornices are richly gilded. But there is not much taste either in the coloring nor the decoration of any church in the hands of the Oriental Christians. Real art after all seems to flourish only where the Catholic church has laid its foundations, and where European influence has been brought to bear. After crossing several paved courts and lanes, we were shown the house of Annas, or rather the church erected upon its site. Here also the Armenian monks were just finishing their services. To the right of the altar they showed a bare niche in the wall in which they claimed Jesus was imprisoned during the night of his trial. Leaving these places, one of the Austrian priests reproached some of the laymen for venerating and kissing the places shown them by the Armenian monks. I loudly protested against his overscrupulousness, maintaining that it is not so much a question of the authenticity of the place, as of the sacred memory connected with it.

We left the Armenian enclosures, which seem to be the most extensive of all those owned by the different divisions of Christians, and proceeded through the gate of Sion to the Cœnaculum. We were cautioned by the guides not to perform any exterior acts of devotion, as the Moslems would make trouble if we did. The pilgrims were not even to go up into the little room where on a former occasion I had seen the bogus tomb of David. Thus the barbaric Turk lords it over the Christians!

Early in the morning after Mass we mounted a pair of asses to ride in the fresh morning air to Bethany. I had some hopes of finding my notebook in the cave of Lazarus. Our search there was in vain, but the old Moslem guide told me that about a hundred French pilgrims had visited the cave yesterday after we had been there. I fondly hoped that I might receive it from one of them later on. But in order not to leave any stone unturned for its recovery, I decided to go as far as the khan of the good Samaritan. So I pursued my way to that place alone, and might have fared just as bad as the wounded man in the parable on this lonely way, if the robbers had only performed their part of the business. Some way or other, however, we missed connections. No trace of the robbers nor of the notebook.

It seems my mule wanted to make up for the loss of incident by an extra display of mulishness. On the way back he began to fall into a snail's pace. Neither the urgings of an impatient tongue, nor the spurring of the heel, or the swishing of the whip would he mind. He insisted on taking the outermost edge of the road, threatening to throw me over the precipice, or, when jerked away, he scraped my knee against the sharp projections of the overhanging rocks on the other side of the road. Then again he would suddenly duck his head and rub his nose against the dusty roadway, almost throwing me over his shoulder. Finally he reached the climax by flopping down with rider and all on the dusty road-bed and refusing to get up in spite of whip and spur. For some time I stood at his side in the mid-day heat perfectly at a loss. The recumbent beast kept wagging his ears in the most nonchalant manner. But there is nothing like a bluff, especially in Turkey, and as an American I thought I would try it on a mule. Going back about twenty paces I spread out my haik and shouting an Indian warwhoop, I rushed upon him with a running jump. Before I landed on his haunches, he had jumped up as if struck by lightning, and, facing around, stared at me with wagging ears. The bluff had worked like a charm.

Doggedly he moved on until we reached a turn in the road. A small distance ahead I saw a dilapidated brother of his lying right in the middle of the road. My mule must have been so busy scheming new rebellion that he did not see his brother ass until he was only a step from him. The other made a feeble effort to rise. Like a blast of gunpowder, mine made a jump into the air, and I, taken unawares, flew into space and landed helter-skelter on the dusty road. He himself stood about five paces away, cocking his ears at his crippled brother. I must have been quite a ludicrous sight in the black haik, streaked with the chalky dust of the road. My long-eared companion seemed to feel himself sufficiently revenged in bringing me to the dust, and without further violence finally brought me home.

CHAPTER XIV.

The Pilgrims' Song — St. Peter's Memory among Protestants — Ain Karem and Surroundings — Golgotha and Environs — Its Complex of Churches — The Rotunda over the Sepulchre — Catholic and Greek Church Near It — Subterranean Chapels — Chapel of the Crucifixion and of the Death of Christ.

I shall never forget the solemn song of the Austrian pilgrims making the Via Dolorosa that evening. I was sitting at the open window and their song echoed along the street outside, suggesting oceans of sorrow. It brought vividly to my mind the song of the pilgrims in the opera of "Die Meistersaenger." I wondered at the similarity of the impressions caused by the fiction in the past and the reality in the present.

The only sacred place which the English-speaking Protestants seem to possess in Jerusalem is the prison where St. Peter was detained by Herod. It belongs to the English mission in the Jewish quarter of Jerusalem. Under one of the buildings, which they use as a printing establishment, is a cellar or vault where the staples are still shown to which the chains of St. Peter, now in Rome, were fastened. This, according to Catholic notions, would be a place well worth keeping in sacred memory. I expected to see some signs of veneration in it, but was sadly disappointed. In the time of the crusaders there was a chapel built over it. In the hands of the Protestants it is turned into a cellar for vegetables. The irons, which once held St. Peter, are now covered with the remains of decaying vegetables, and the other parts of the prison adjoining are used for a wood-shed. A Moslem is too lazy to keep sacred places free from dirt, and his religion does not allow him any profuse decorations, but he will never permit such a place to be put to profane use, and he will make you take off your shoes before entering. No such regard is paid by the English Protestant. St. Peter was no war hero or great statesman of theirs. In Cawnpore, they have built a grand monument over the well in which some of the victims of their war of conquest were thrown. They made us talk in a whisper in the park surrounding it. Thousands of places are adorned with monuments and memorial churches, and consume millions yearly in their preservation. Here in Jerusalem the English Protestants happen to be in possession of just one place of sacred memory, and this they leave in a most shameful condition of neglect. I say this in no bitterness, but only in order to give vent to my feeling of regret that Saint Peter's memory should be thus loaded with insult. Do Protestants owe nothing to Saint Peter, the head of the apostles?

In the morning of the last Sunday of our stay in Jerusalem, Mahomet, our favorite driver, stood ready with his carriage in order to take us out to Ain Karem, the birthplace of St. John and the scene of the visitation of the Blessed Virgin. Lustily he rattled on to the gate of Damascus, scattering the laggard foot-passengers to right and left. A few miles out the scenery becomes quite pleasing, especially toward the valley that runs in the direction of Bethlehem. The road winds down the hillside, supported by a high embankment, and Ain Karem presented a very cheerful sight, with its neat houses, its eight or ten churches, some of them over-topped by high steeples. On the spot where Mary first met Elizabeth on her visit, the Franciscans are in charge of a fine church and monastery. High mass was going

ENTRANCE — THE HOLY SEPULCHRE — INTERIOR

on when we entered. At the end a procession with the blessed Sacrament was held, in which the natives joined, singing the Te Deum in Arabic. To the left of the high altar is the crypt and sanctuary, the meeting place of the Mother of God with her cousin Elizabeth. Here for the first time resounded the sublimest of all anthems, the Magnificat, and from that blessed tongue, which also first made our Salvation secure by accepting the proposals of the heavenly father.

Farther down in the valley the road passes a picturesque fountain that sends forth an abundant stream. Beyond, on the opposite hill, a new chapel and convent is built upon the excavated walls of older structures, marking the birthplace of St. John. Next to the altar in the chapel is the well of St. Elizabeth, of miraculous origin, and, in an opening in the wall to the right, a small cave is shown as the hiding place of St. John and his mother during the slaughter of the innocents by Herod. The cliffs overhanging the convent are honeycombed by old burying places. Some of them, now sealed up again, contain the remains of recently deceased Franciscans. Ain Karem itself does not make the woebegone impression which many of the other places of Palestine invariably make upon the visitor. Most of the inhabitants are Christians, as in Bethlehem and Nazareth. Our visit to this place was one of the most enjoyable in Palestine.

The most remarkable place in Jerusalem and, for that matter, in the whole world, will always remain the Holy Sepulchre. Of course we visited this place often during our stay of a month, but we spent one day in making a thorough inspection of the extensive buildings connected with it. The church of the Holy Sepulchre is on the hill to the north of Mount Sion. At the time of Christ this hill was outside the then existing walls of the city. In later times the present walls were built in a wide sweep around the hill of Golgotha, thus making it part of the city. The new addition to the city was densely populated and the present church, though built on a hill, is almost hidden in a cluster of the other high buildings. It is well known that the church of the Holy Sepulchre is really a group of churches and chapels, which form one whole, covering both the burial place of our Lord and the hill on which he was crucified. That is easily possible, since they are only about a hundred feet apart. Golgotha was only a small hillock, and may be called a part of Mt. Sion. At its foot and into the rocky sides of the hill Joseph of Arimathea had built a sepulchre for himself, into which he helped to place the Savior with his own hand. St. Helena, the mother of the Emperor Constantine, before she built the church over the grave, leveled the rocks around it, cutting away also a large portion of the rock of Golgotha.

Thus a level space of about seventy feet in diameter was created, on which the great rotunda of the church now stands. She even went so far as to cut away the vestibule of the original tomb, leaving only a sort of shell, which to this day vaults over the resting place of Jesus. The whole of this is covered by a marble structure about fifteen feet long and ten wide, surmounted by a Byzantine cupola. The whole monument is probably not over twenty feet high. In the front, a small door opens into a sort of vestibule, which is called the Chapel of the Angel; for here the angel sat upon a stone when the pious women paid their visit to the grave. In the rear of this vestibule there is a hole in the monument so narrow that only an ordinary sized person could squeeze through, and so low that only a child of ten years could enter in upright position. This aperture gives admission to the real tomb of our Lord. However, nothing of it can be seen except the bare rocks above, all black from the smoke of the lamps, and a marble slab

about six feet long and two broad, which forms an altar-
table across the niche in the wall. Beneath this slab is
the native rock, chiseled out for a resting place of the
human body. There lay the sacred body of Christ until
the third day. Above the altar-table are some rich
ornaments, and several lamps of precious metal. On
that marble slab, just above the spot where the divine
Savior rested in death, I celebrated holy mass in Easter
week, as I have already mentioned. In the narrow
vault, perhaps not more than five or six persons would
find room to stand. The Greeks have cut holes through
the rock on top in order to give egress to the smoke of
the perpetual lamps. They have also cut an oval hole
into each side of the vestibule or chapel of the angel in
order to hand out their sacred fire on Holy Saturday.
The Russian people are made to believe that the fire
descends direct from heaven on Easter night.

Above the sepulchral monument the great rotunda
of the church rises to a height of over a hundred and
fifty feet. The pillars or ribs of the rotunda rise straight
to the curve and then all unite in the centre of the
cupola. The architecture is Byzantine and the rotunda
is common ground for all the different denominations
of Christians; but the hours during which services may
be held in the Sepulchre are strictly regulated. On
the outside, to the rear part of the monument, is
attached the altar of the Copts. The spaces between
the pillars and the outside wall of the rotunda form a
circular row of chapels belonging to different denominations. One of them, opposite the Coptic altar, is
held as a chapel for the Syrians, and in a recess of that
chapel is the tomb of Joseph of Arimathea.

In order that the reader may obtain some idea of
the location of the other important points of the great
church, let him start with me from the Austrian hospice
on a tour of exploration. Coming up from the hospice,

and passing the remains of the old city gate built before the time of Christ, we happen upon one of the most lively bazaar streets of Jerusalem. It winds somewhat around the foot of the hill of Golgotha. At the next corner we will turn to the right about one hundred and fifty paces. We have been going up hill a little and skirted Golgotha on its east and south side. Now we stand before a narrow entrance to a court paved with flag-stones, and opposite to us is the portal of a church. Nothing is seen of this church except the facade, like a ruin among ruins. On each side of us old convent buildings hide the rest of the church and form the limits of the courtyard. Entering the portals of the facade we pass a bevy of Turkish soldiers lying on a rug-covered platform to our left.

Ahead of us we see a jumble of pillars; to the right of them there seems to be a chapel raised about twenty-five feet above our standing ground. This is the summit of Golgotha, which has been cut into a cubic form. We walk straight ahead for ten steps and stand before a large stone slab, surrounded by a railing. The pilgrims kneel down and kiss it, for it is the stone on which the body of Christ was anointed for burial. To our left, ahead of us, between two of the great pillars of the rotunda, our eyes are caught by the gleam of many lights. They are the lights of the Holy Sepulchre. Around the Sepulchre is a free circular space over which rises the rotunda. There are sixteen of the pillars, but they do not complete the circle. The whole width of the rotunda, opposite the entrance of the Sepulchre, forms a high and sweeping arch, opening into a large church now in possession of the Russians or Greeks. If we pass on to the left around the tomb, that is, on the side which is opposite to the Russian church, we pass between the Coptic altar and the Syrian chapel. Following the circle around so as to complete a half circuit, we see behind the pillars an altar to the right. It is the place where our Lord appeared to Magdalen as she stood weeping.

But we must look farther in that direction, for there is a door a few steps beyond that altar, and it seems to open into a chapel. So it does: as we enter we see the familiar decorations and arrangements of Catholic churches. The richly decorated altar in the middle commemorates the spot where the risen Savior appeared to the women; the one to the right contains, behind a screen, the column of the flagellation, the one to the left contains other relics. Adjoining this chapel is the dwelling of the Franciscans, who attend to the service and are imprisoned there during the night.

Now we must return again to the rotunda and continue our circuit. Immediately in front of the Sepulchre, as already mentioned, is the entrance to the Russian church, which is the largest of the chapels and the most beautifully decorated of the whole complex of buildings. On the mosaic pavement, in the centre, a stone, in the shape of a knob, projects. Russian pilgrims are continually kneeling down beside it to cover it with kisses, for their papas tell them that it is the navel of the whole world. In front rises the magnificent iconostasis, hiding the inner sanctuary. The iconostasis in Greek churches is a partition to conceal the sanctuary and the priest during some parts of the mass. In the middle of it is an arched door, through which, when open, the altar is seen; on each side of this door are ornaments; above it is generally the picture of the Virgin, and on each side of this picture are the paintings of four saints. Running along the walls, on each side of the main body of this church, are stalls or partitioned seats for the monks. The walls and ceilings above them are beautifully frescoed, though of course in Byzantine style. Behind the iconostasis, precious metal and jeweled mosaics glitter in profusion on the altar and on the walls. Behind the altar is the magnificent throne of the Greek patriarch.

We can pass out of the sanctuary of the Greek or Russian church through a small door on the left. We are then in the open passageway between the church and an old convent, between which two mighty and shapeless pillars support the roof above. In front of us to the right, thirty steps ahead, a dark recess in the corner of the wall, contains an altar. It is the cave into which Jesus was thrown, while the executioners prepared the cross. We come back almost to the door of the Greek sanctuary and enter a passage leading behind it. In niches to the left is the altar of Longinus and of the division of the garments of Christ. Farther on we enter an underground passage to our left, and in the dim background of the expanding cavern, we see the flickering light of candles. They are burning on the altars about thirty feet away from us in the chapel of St. Helena. On descending about forty steps hewn down into the rock, we find it to be a very roomy cave, but entirely bare and neglected except for three rude altars. The chapel belongs to the Armenians. The candles have probably been placed there by some devout pilgrims of a different denomination. But some faint glimmer of lighted candles seems to come from the rear right-hand corner. Accordingly we descend through the narrow passage on twenty more rough steps, and arrive in a small cave, where likewise candles are burning on a rude altar. This is the cave where the true cross was found with the crosses of the two thieves. It belongs to the Latins. The rock is left in its natural condition, and is all blackened with smoke.

On leaving these caves and returning up the two stairs, we land again in the passage behind the Greek church and continuing around the rear of its sanctuary we pass a niche to our left containing the altar of the Column of

Mockery. Only a few steps farther a narrow stone stairs leads down into some chambers, which have been dug out under the very hill of Calvary, and are used by the Greek monks. Only about thirty feet farther in the passage (having walked completely around the rear of the sanctuary of the Greek church) we come to a narrow stairway, which seems to lead up about twenty feet along what seems a wall. This wall is nothing else than the natural rock of Calvary, the slope of which has been thus cut down perpendicularly by St. Helena. Above the edge of it the pillars of a chapel rise, and we can see the decorations on the ceiling about thirty feet from our floor. If we wish, we can climb these stairs (which belong to the Greeks) and see the chapels on Golgotha, but we prefer first to pass around these stairs to the left, and come to a door in the face of the rocky wall. It leads into the chapel of Adam. Tradition says, that in a cave immediately under the cross of our Savior, the bones of Adam were found. The Greeks have made a chapel of it. Around it are also some other chambers, where if you pry about, the Greek papas will soon give you to understand that you are not wanted. Within this chapel you stand almost beneath the exact spot where Jesus expired on the cross.

But come out, for the papas are scowling at you even more than in other portions of the building. They know that they have nothing to expect of such unorthodox Christians as we are. Outside the door we continue our way, and find a stone stairs winding upward in an angle formed by the wall of Calvary and that of the vestibule. We might as well ascend the stairs; it is the Latin one, leading up to Golgotha. As we reach the top we see two chapels, divided only by two pillars running lengthwise between them. The one in which the stairs end is the Latin chapel of the crucifixion; the other to our left is the Greek chapel of the death of Christ. In the first one, immediately in front of us, the mosaic pavement shows the figure of a cross; there Jesus lay stretched out on the real cross, and while He was being nailed to it by three long spikes driven through hands and feet. It was done in such a cruel manner that all the joints of His arms and limbs were dislocated. Imagine how that gang of executioners must have pulled and tugged at those unresisting limbs in order to wrench them so far apart. Remember also, if you like, that it was done for your benefit and mine. In front is the altar, which commemorates this dreadful nailing to the cross. Aside of it, to the left, is a smaller altar with the statue of the Mater Dolorosa; there Mary stood, when the quivering limbs of Jesus were being nailed to the cross, and there she stood during the three hours, while He hung upon it in agony. Who is so stony-hearted as not to be moved by the woe of such a Mother!

But we pass between the pillar and this statue to our left to the chapel of the death of Christ. The Greeks are jealously watching our motions, as we stand before the altar. A lifesize silver crucifix is fixed into the native rock at our feet. Costly lamps and candlesticks and the statue of the holy women on each side adorn the altar. From the ceiling is suspended a magnificent hanging lamp, in which colored lights are burning. A portion of the bare rock immediately around the cross is uncovered, and about three feet from the foot is the opening of a large crack in the rock, which originated at the death of Christ. At the moment of his death the earth shook in her foundations, the rock of Calvary split between the cross of Christ and that of the impenitent thief, and the dead arose from their graves. How these happenings must have frightened the inhabitants of Jerusalem! Yet what happened then is only a slight foreshadowing of the terrors that will invade the earth on the last day. At that time God wished only to warn those who were well disposed; the terrors of the last day are for those who have despised all his commands and all his kindness. We have now seen the whole of the church of the Holy Sepulchre; let us say a prayer at the Sepulchre, and leave the church, esteeming ourselves singularly favored in having been permitted to walk through these most sacred places.

CHAPTER XV.

With the Austrians to Mt. Moria — Green-Mantled Hadshi — In Omar Mosque — The Hadshi's Brazen Statements — Oriental Splendor — In El Akseh — A Fat Man's Predicament — Stables of Solomon — In Bethlehem — Basilicas and Caves — Shepherds' Field and the Milk-Cave — Desperate Plans — Happy Expedient — Practical Hints.

On one of the last days of our stay we accompanied the Austrian pilgrims on their visit to Mount Moria and the temple grounds. These grounds are surrounded on all four sides by walls some thirty feet high. The length of the grounds is about half a mile and their breadth one quarter of a mile. It is a plateau half covered with rank, untrimmed grass. In the middle rises the beautiful Omar mosque, and on the south end of the plateau the vast basilica of El Akseh spreads out over the vaults of Solomon. On the east, near the Golden gate, is an octagonal kiosk, and along the west and north walls run porticos, some of them walled up to serve for habitations of those in charge of the grounds. Here also is the dwelling of the pasha, which is surrounded by a high minaret.

On our entrance we were taken in tow by a gaunt, green-mantled and green-turbaned Arab. This is the dress worn by the hadshis, or those who have made the pilgrimage to Mecca. But when I asked him later on, whether he had made that pilgrimage, he answered with infinite disdain, that this place is Mecca enough. Although none among the pilgrims besides ourselves understood English, he began to sputter away his Moslemite information in horridly butchered fragments of English, so that the Germans were only at a small disadvantage in comparison with ourselves. The substructure of the Omar mosque is an octagonal of the most graceful proportions, and the beautiful cupola rises above it to the height of some two hundred feet. The material seems to be a gray limestone, darkened by age. The sides are broken by sculptured panels, within which are the Moorish windows arranged in pairs. There are four portals on each of the four larger sides.

Having covered our feet with clumsy overshoes, we entered on the west side. In the middle an irregularly shaped rock, some fifty feet in diameter, rose to the height of about eight feet. It is entirely bare and surrounded by a circular railing of equal height. Beautifully proportioned pillars circle around this rock and aspire to the cupola. The railing runs from pillar to pillar in graceful arabesque and trellis work. This rock is the summit of Mount Moria, where Abraham had intended to sacrifice his son. The hadshi showed us some circular holes in its edge, saying that they are the fingermarks of the angel Gabriel. Mahomet, he said, came to this rock with El Borak, his heavenly steed, in order to ascend into heaven to the throne of Allah. But even the mountains felt the effects of the trance in which Mahomet fell at the moment of ascending. When the prophet began to ascend, the rock of Moria clung to the feet of El Borak to accompany the prophet. Probably Allah considered this an unnecessary baggage, which would retard the journey. So he sent the angel Gabriel in order to hold the unruly mountain in its place. The fearful grasp of the angel caused his fingers to bury themselves into the rock, thus causing the small holes. The hadshi told us this story with the most solemn face, and moreover tried to make us believe that this rock is in no wise connected with the rest of the mountain, but remains suspended some ten feet in mid-air; namely, in the very place which it had already reached before the angel came to stop its yearning flight. Of course none of us giaours dared to misbelieve the story. A hadshi can't tell any lies. But I must say, that I might possibly have believed somewhat more implicitly, if I had been able to see the empty space under the great rock. It was a pity that the four-foot wall running all around it prevented us from verifying the fact. I hope the reader will also be satisfied with the word of the saintly hadshi.

The great cupola is directly above this rock, resting on the rotunda of beautiful pillars. Its ceiling is richly gilded. At about half the height of the rotunda the substructure spreads away all around in eight octagonal sections. The gilding, the mosaic and trellis work on the ceilings and walls of the encircling lower structure, are exquisitely artistic. Our hadshi now brought us to the south side and showed us an ordinary cave underneath the great rock. The sides of this cave were covered with marble slabs, but above us were some projections. He said they marked the places where Abraham, Moses, Elias, and other great saints had forced their way out of this cave, as soon as Mahomet had emigrated to the better world. Every soul, too, that is destined for heaven is kept prisoner in this cave, until it can force an opening through the solid rock above. I wonder what all the millions of Mahometan souls thought of the saintly hadshi for introducing so many giaours into their narrow abode. Perhaps they stepped out through the open door of their prison, just for a change, until the cursed giaours should again vacate their prison; some of them may even never have returned to bore their way to heaven through the rock.

I wished also the hadshi had pointed out the empty space under the great rock, of which he had so glibly informed us when speaking of the archangel's fingerholes. We were under it now, but as far as we could see, without appearing too inquisitive, the rock rested on a mighty solid foundation. But then what right had we unbelieving giaours to pry so closely into the mysteries of the Haram es Sherif?

The Omar mosque occupies the site of the Temple of Solomon. The rock probably supported the sanctuary, or holy of holies, of the God of Israel. On the spacious grounds outside, the pious Moslem pilgrims as they approached, showed their reverence in many ways, now kneeling down, now raising their arms in supplication, now prostrating themselves in the direction of the mosque. About one hundred feet in front of each of the four portals, at the foot of a gently rising terrace, four pillared arches guard the approaches.

Our hadshi with his flowing mantle preceded us to the mosque El Akseh on the south end of the temple plateau. This building is much larger than the Omar mosque, as it was originally the great five-naved basilica built by the crusaders on the site of Solomon's palaces. Its shape and architecture, being basilican, is in strange contrast to its present use. The Turks keep this and the Omar mosque in fair condition, which is rarely the case with other mosques in the Turkish Empire. As one enters the main portals, two rows of huge Doric pillars stretch away to the front, carrying the high middle nave. Its ceiling rises nearly twice the height of the four other naves. The pavement is not in very good condition; part of it is covered with old carpets.

A dervish sat in the rear of the left sidenave, surrounded by a circle of Moslems. He was explaining the Koran. Our hadshi brought us to the front and sung the praises of the mihrab, or front niche, and of the great pulpit carved from olive wood. Much finer ones had we seen in India. The pillars, which formerly divided the sanctuary from the left wing of the church, are so closely placed together, that a stout man could not pass between them. The belief was current, that whoever could manage to squeeze through between these pillars, would also be certain of passing through the gate of paradise. Some time ago a fat Mahometan dignitary, wishing to gain this certainty, stuck fast between these pillars, so that they had to cut out his body. In order to prevent any more blocking up of heaven's gateways by carrion flesh, the spaces between the pillars are now walled up. The mosque El Akseh seems bare and cheerless, for all the decorations that savor of Christianity are daubed over with dull paint. We descended into the subterranean crypt, and wondered at the huge blocks of stone which form the foundation of the basilica. Parts of the foundations date back to Solomon's time.

In fact the entire southern end of the temple-ground is really a platform, which rests on the massive vaults built up from the gentle slope of the hillside. On the southeast corner of the city walls, which is at the same time the southeast corner of the temple-grounds, a passage leads down underneath this platform. The corridors between the vaulted columns that bear the platform are called the stables of Solomon. In some places the iron rings and the stone cribs for the horses are still traceable. Solomon must have had little objection to the smell of ammonia usually connected with stables of horses, for his palaces were built above these vaults. The masonry of these vaults, which cover seven acres of the hillslope, has withstood the wear of three thousand years, and it is apparently as solid as when first erected. A few openings in the south wall admit some light, but the rear vaults are in darkness.

Coming again to daylight our hadshi led the way along the east wall to the Golden gate. This is built of marble and the inside forms a vestibule with some exquisitely carved pillars. The gate is said to have been built by Solomon, but it must be of much later date. It has been walled up ever since the Moslems obtained possession of Jerusalem. The Turks firmly believe that this is the only vulnerable place in Jerusalem and that here the enemy will enter, if Jerusalem ever falls into the hands of the Christians. A fair-sized modern cannon ball from the Russian hospice on the west side of the city could pave its way through the whole city of Jerusalem, to this gate, smash it to atoms and chip off some splinters from the rocks of Mount Olivet across the valley of Josaphat. What infatuation to think that walling up this gate should save this city from invasion! Near this gate is a small octagonal structure of white marble, in which the Moslems claim to have in preservation the throne of Solomon. As we were walking over the uncut grass toward the northwest entrance of the temple square, the muezzins were calling out their "Allah il Allah." The only minaret on these grounds is the graceful stone tower that rises like a slender, graceful column, 150 feet above the dwelling of the pasha. It occupies the northwest corner of the temple plateau. The turbaned muezzins looked like boys moving around the minaret and calling out their summons as if from the blue sky. Their clear voices, mingling with those from other minarets in Jerusalem and re-echoing through the evening air, seemed like a reminder to many a Christian of his duty to pray. This at least is an admirable institution of Mahomet, that his followers are reminded so often of Allah and of their duty to seek his blessings.

Next morning found us in Bethlehem. There being no opportunity of soon saying mass on the altar of the crib, I said it on the altar of St. Joseph, next to the cave of the Nativity. The Russians were having their services at the altar of the Nativity. It consisted of interminable singing in long-drawn notes. The celebrant and his assistants in colored vestments and moving about in the cave, sang endless responses, frequently using incense. After they had finished, we made the tour of inspection of the caves and of the church. A few stairs in the rock lead down directly into the cave of the Nativity. This is about thirty by ten feet, the floor paved in mosaics, but the bare rocks forming the vault about eight feet high. A Turkish soldier guards the entrance day and night. The altar of the Nativity is only three steps from the entrance in the front wall. A silver star, in the marble slab under the altar, marks the precise spot of the birth of Christ. This altar belongs to the Greeks. On the other side of the stairs is a smaller cave, forming a sort of alcove. It belongs to the Latins and contains two altars; one on the place where the three kings adored the Child, the other where the Child rested in the manger. Opposite this alcove is the stairs leading up into the Greek or Russian convent.

Passing through the length of the larger cave, we come to a miraculous well in one corner and to a narrow passage on the other. This passage leads into the cave of St. Joseph. An altar occupies the spot where Joseph received the message of the angel, bidding him arise from sleep and fly into Egypt. Next to this cave is the cave of the holy Innocents. Their altar stands over a deep cavity in the floor, into which many bodies of the slaughtered Innocents were thrown. From this cave there are two different passages; one leads up into the church of St. Catherine in charge of the Franciscans, the other leads into another cave. In this cave there are three altars: the altar of St. Eusebius, of St. Paula and Eustochium, and of St. Jerome. All these saints have spent a good part of their lives in these caves. Still another and larger cave is connected with the one last named, and was the habitation of St. Jerome for many years.

We must now go back to the cave of the Innocents in

order to pass up the stone stairs in to the church of St. Catherine. Let the reader understand, that there are three entrances to the caves, and that two churches are built aside of each other above these caves; two entrances connect with the churches, and one with the street. The older of the two churches is the basilica of the Nativity, which dates back to the time of St. Helena, and is now in the hands of the Russians. The body of this church contains five naves, resting on four rows of doric pillars. So little do the Greeks or Russian, care for the venerable building, which they stole from the Franciscans, that they allow a public market to be held in its main part; the sanctuary they have partitioned off and use for their parochial church. On each side of the middle of this sanctuary, about thirty-five feet apart, are two stairs, both leading directly to the grotto and altar of the Nativity. Behind and aside of the basilica, on the right as we face the altar, are convents of the Greek and Armenian monks. On the left of the ancient church of the Nativity adjoins the church of St. Catherine and the Franciscan monasteries and schools. Near the portals of this church is a passage underground leading directly to the caves of the holy Innocents and of St. Joseph, which connect it with the cave of the Nativity. The church of St. Catherine is only three-naved and only half as long as the basilica of the Nativity. Both these churches are so hidden by the adjoining convents, that nothing except the belfry of St. Catherine is prominent to view outside. We had a whole case of devotional articles brought into the cave of the Nativity and laid on the holy places, in order to serve as mementoes to our friends on our return. One of the Franciscan fathers blessed these articles and attached to them the great indulgences.

Afterwards a guide took us about a mile and a half down into the valley of the shepherds. Here the angelic hosts appeared to the simple shepherds to announce the birth of Christ. The precise spot of their appearance is a grotto under the vaulted ruins of an old church. It is in the possession of the Greeks and they keep it in their own neglectful way. They have, however, put a fence around the place and demand a bakshish from visitors. Nothing is to be seen inside except crumbling stones and dirt. On our return we made a detour to the southwest side of Bethlehem, where, on a high hill, is the Milk-grotto. Here the Blessed Virgin stayed for a short time with the Child. A miraculous spring welled from the solid rock, where, as tradition says, some of the Virgin's milk dropped, while she was nursing the Infant Jesus. The Franciscans have transformed the grotto and its surroundings into a beauty spot. The interior is richly decorated and several lights burn continually on the marble altar. A garden filled with an abundance of flowers befittingly enclosed the grotto. Pilgrims generally take along some of the limestone ground, baked into pellets, which is said to be of wonderful efficacy in curing the ailments of child-bearing women. The streets of Bethlehem, though narrow and irregular, have an air of business about them. The people seem to be more prosperous and of higher type than those generally met with in Jerusalem and Palestine. The principal industry is the manufacture of devotional articles. Having packed our goods in a box ready for shipment at Dabdoub's store, we brought it to Jerusalem, and shipped it to New York through Singer's express agency.

We had spent about a month in the Holy Land and it was time for us to look for passage on some out-bound vessel in Jaffa. But an unexpected difficulty arose: quarantine had been declared against all vessels from eastern ports. Hence, on all such vessels, we were liable to quarantine on arrival in European or Turkish ports. Besides, no steamer was due at Jaffa within the next few weeks. I had already urgently requested the manager of the Austrian pilgrimage to be permitted to take passage on their chartered steamer. But they had given me small hope, claiming that their steamer was overcrowded, and that they were afraid of difficulties on landing at Triest, if they brought passengers not belonging to the pilgrimage. As the season was far advanced, it would be a great hardship to lose at least ten days in quarantine. We thought ourselves somewhat ill used by the refusal of the Austrian pilgrims to take us aboard. Hence we had made up our minds to smuggle ourselves aboard the ship with the crowd of pilgrims and see what would come of the matter later on. They could take their choice, either to accept pay for the voyage, or else throw us overboard, like Jonah of old, who played a similar trick in the very same port. At any rate, we were prepared to take the risk and treatment of stow-aways, rather than be delayed by quarantine.

In order to put our desperate plan into execution it was necessary to be on hand on the morning when the pilgrims were to embark on the Poseidon. Accordingly we took the morning train for Jaffa on the day before. At the Franciscan hospice in Jaffa, we found four of the Austrian pilgrims, two of them very sick. They readily promised to co-operate in our scheme; for we did not tell them of the scanty encouragement which the managers of the pilgrimage had given us on applying for passage. As we would probably have to sleep on deck during our passage, we bought two woolen blankets in one of the bazaars. A Christian native of the hospice had accompanied us on this purchase, and he naturally inquired about the use we intended to make of the blankets. When we had explained to him, that we would probably need them for sleeping on deck of the Poseidon, he asked us why we did not take the Aphrodite to Constantinople, instead of crowding ourselves on board the pilgrim ship.

The Aphrodite was a small steamer anchored in the harbor, of which the brother in the hospice had told us that it was bound for Alexandria, just the place which we wanted to avoid on account of the quarantine. How glad we were to find, that she was to depart that day, not for Alexandria, but for Constantinople, and that she would nowhere be subject to quarantine, since she had not touched at any Egyptian port. On my getting aboard the Aphrodite, the captain accompanied me to the shore and procured tickets to Constantinople at a greatly reduced rate. We paid only eighty francs for two first cabin tickets to Constantinople. Having sold our blankets again to the very merchant from whom we had bought them, we now looked to the arrival of the Austrian pilgrims with great equanimity.

At about nine o'clock they came trooping along from the depot in irregular groups and began entering the small boats in great confusion. The Poseidon was riding at anchor half a mile out beyond the dangerous rocks inshore. The embarking of the pilgrims took nearly two hours and from the high balcony of the hospice it presented a very lively scene. With some of the last stragglers I boarded the pilgrim ship and saw her whole interior honeycombed with rude berths. I then realized how fortunate we had been in procuring passage on the other vessel. My desire had been to see Constantinople; now, instead of going direct to Triest, we would be able to visit several of the historic islands and sea-coast cities of the Mediterranean, and of Syria and Asiatic Turkey, and, in easy stages, finally reach Constantinople.

Proudly the great pilgrim ship, with booming cannons, flying pennants, and martial music moved away into the Mediterranean, and from the balcony of the hospice we waved the inmates a friendly adieu. The Poseidon dwindled more and more into the distance and finally disappeared beneath the dark-blue horizon. We ourselves embarked on the trim Aphrodite at four o'clock, and a few hours later the ship weighed anchor, carrying us away from the shores of the Holy Land. Blessed are the days we spent there, full of pleasing and consoling memories. "Si oblitus fuero tui Jerusalem oblivioni detur dextera mea; adhaereat lingua mea faucibus meis, si non meminero tui: si non proposuero Jerusalem in principio laetitiae meae." "If I forget thee, Jerusalem, may my right hand be given to oblivion; let my tongue cleave to my mouth, if I am not mindful of thee; if I do not place Jerusalem in the beginning of my joy."

PRACTICAL HINTS. In regard to the traditions connected with the holy places in Palestine, it is good to exercise some judgment. The most reliable source of information is the Catholic church, and especially the Franciscan order. The Catholic church has always shown pious interest in the places connected with the doings of biblical personages, and therefore she was the faithful custodian of the holy places, just as she has been the only custodian of the Sacred Scriptures. The Mahometans have so mixed their fables with holy persons and places, that practically nothing reliable concerning the original history remains to them. The schismatic Greeks, Armenians, Copts, Syrians, never did enter into the spirit of the traditions which they received from the mother church, and therefore much of their information is distorted and full of errors. The importance of the principal facts connected with a place is very often minimized in favor of minor circumstances bearing out their schismatic doctrines.

Since the twelfth century the Franciscans were the sole custodians of holy places and of their traditions. They have spent large sums of money for excavations, and in many places historic accounts are still extant dating back many centuries. Ever since St. Francis visited the Orient the custody of the Holy Land is intimately interwoven with the whole history of their order. Hence there is no doubt that their information is the most reliable. From this it follows, that the most advantageous places to take lodging are their hospices in the different parts of Palestine. Those that make a longer stay in the Holy Land, should guard against a sickness which sometimes besets pilgrims. It is a peculiar sort of fever, the nature of which is not known and is called Jerusalem fever. Residents there may have some remedies against it, but after it has once taken a good hold, the only safety is to depart as soon as possible.

CHAPTER XVI.

LIBANUS MOUNT — HIGH WORDS AT LOW INSINUA-
TIONS — NEAR ANTIOCH — IN TARSUS OF CILI-
CIA — RHODES AND CHIOS.

Jaffa, rising like a hemisphere of white buildings from either side of the shore, was a long time in sight, but gradually the widening distance and the gathering dusk hid it and the adjoining hills from view. The morning of Thursday, May 10th, found us on the calm, sunny ocean off the coast of Beirut. Hermon's snowy top, 9,500 feet high, glittered like a giant over the Libanus range along the Syrian shore.

At table the few passengers entered freely into conversation. Among them was a lady, Mrs. Hanson, who seemed to be some kind of reporter for a periodical in England. She was accompanied by an Arab dragoman and his son, a native of Ramallah, the town I failed to find on my trip to Nazareth. The captain spoke some English, he and the other officers, and three or four passengers, were Greeks. As the lady began to talk about seasickness, I remarked, that while affected with it, one does not know whether the next lurch of the vessel would throw one into the bottom of hell, or send him up to heaven, altogether unprepared for enjoyment, so undefined was the feeling it is apt to cause. The strong comparison at once brought the dragoman to introduce religion. I have always noticed, that there is no surer way to stir up religious discussion, than to merely hint at hell. In so-called polite society, no mention must be made of hell. It touches everybody to the quick, which no doubt is a proof, that the dim fear of hell is in every human breast, and is in itself a cogent proof of the existence of hell. Else why such sensitiveness?

Without any introduction the dragoman asked me pointedly, whether I was not a Catholic priest. Yes, of course. Why do Catholic priests demand money for absolving sins, and why do they claim to be able to liberate souls from purgatory for stipulated sums of money? This was a little too much for my equanimity. I spoiled some of his barefaced assurance, by telling him that any one who claimed to be able to prove that assertion was a liar.. I felt a twinge of conscience for having used so strong a term at table and before ladies, but once having made the sally, which the occasion perhaps justified, I bombarded him with what easily came to hand just then. He shielded himself by saying that many people had told him so. His informers were relegated to the aforesaid class of individuals. All the priests in the world could not change the fate of any soul, if money were to be used as motive power. But Catholics believe and know the efficacy of prayer and sacrifice offered for such souls as were suffering in purgatory. Hence they ask the intercession of the priest as minister of God, not only for themselves, but for their deceased friends. To accept payment for giving absolution, for indulgences, masses, or prayers is branded by the church as Simony and is punished in the severest manner. Every Catholic understands this and they are the last to offer any payment for spiritual favors. The gifts offered on such occasions are looked upon as contributions either toward the building and maintenance of churches and schools, or for the support of the pastors. Why should that, which is freely done in every religious denomination all over the world and in every profession, be a crime only in the Catholic church? Besides, no money is ever offered for confession or absolution. As the dragoman was not a revengeful or malicious man, only a great talker, we were soon on good terms again and remained so during the voyage.

No very strict separation was kept between first and second class passengers on the Greek vessel. Some Greek papas in second class, were with the first class passengers most of the time. We were glad to have calm weather, for as the Aphrodite was not a large vessel, we would have been thrown about considerably in a rough sea. Moonlight lay over the rippling sea and over the distant Libanus, that hides the historic plains of Damascus. Snow gleamed between some of the bare mountain-crags, while at their base dark streaks marked the woody slopes and green fields along the shore. Early in the morning we entered the bay of Iskenderoum or ancient Antioch. The city itself is in ruins and replaced by a small town called Antaka. At Alexandretta where Alexander gained his first decisive victory on his march to Persia, the Turkish harbor-officials surprised us by their polite and reasonable reception on landing. We walked through the cobble-stone streets of Alexandretta, past many shops, that had a businesslike air about them, to the Catholic church in charge of the Carmelites. One of the fathers sat in a forlorn schoolroom, waiting for his laggard scholars to appear. He told us that the trip to the ruins of Antioch would take two days, but one could get a distant view of the surroundings, from a mountain-pass behind Bela, ten miles from here. The excursion to the mountain-pass would in itself be a very pleasant ride. Thereupon we concluded, if possible, to secure conveyance to Bela.

A boy conducted us to a large khan, and, as we pretended not to be so very anxious, we soon got offers of a carriage for a reasonable price. But our driver this time was not Mahomet, of Jerusalem. After making a spurt out of town, he and his horses seemed bent on sleep more than on making any particular headway. They slowly crawled up the gentle slopes, which descended from the rugged mountains to the sea. We were not sorry, for the scenery became more and more charming. As we passed through a rocky gorge, Bela lay before us crouched up in the angle of two adjoining mountains. The roofs of its houses were made of dark-colored tile, and looked like irregular black terraces at the head of the mountain gulch. Mountains clad in verdure hemmed us in on three sides as we climbed farther up, while to the rear of us, northwest of Alexandretta, the great Taurus range stretched away like vast western continents. Southward of the mountains, far out in the blue ocean, the hazy cliffs of the island of Cyprus are visible. A comparatively fine pike road winds through the mountain-pass; it is maintained by the toll receipts.

The inhabitants of Bela mustered us closely, though not uncivilly. Their appearance was that of well-to-do and independent people; no beggars were met with. There is a pretty strong sprinkling of Druses among them; many of these could be seen in the street in their gaudy and snug-fitting garments. They seem a stalwart and hardy race. The shops and houses have an appearance of prosperity and enterprise about them, quite different from those in Palestine.

After about two miles of further climbing we arrived at the mountain-pass, from whence the road again descends to distant plains. To the left the plains are much broken up by lakes and marshes, while on the verges of the plain to the right the ruins of Antioch were dimly visible. A spur of hills intercepts the view of the village of Antaka. From the heights on which we stood, the army of Alexander may have viewed Antioch from afar, or the crusaders, in their weary march, may have been gladdened by the sight of the rich plains and the prospect of glorious contest against the Moslem hosts gathered together in Antioch.

On our return the driver had accepted as a companion, a Druse lad of about sixteen years. Though he was but a poor mountaineer, he had a fine and noble bearing about him. Half way down, our driver, having noticed that we took some interest in the flowers that grew in profusion on the mountain slopes, decorated the horses and the carriage with huge bushes of yellow blossoms. We rode into Alexandretta in gala style; however laggard the pace had been uphill, our driver, on approaching the town, lashed the horses into a furious gallop. Our carriage was in danger of being knocked to splinters on the rough boulders, and we ourselves, of landing in some hole along the wayside. But if reckless, he was an expert driver, and no accident happened.

Not a single hint was given us on leaving the custom pier, that a bakshish was expected. We mentally scored a point in favor of the harbor officials of Alexandretta. Our good ship resumed her voyage, and now headed southwestward in order to clear the great promontory of Asia Minor. The silvery sheen of the moon glittered in the wake of the vessel, and our quibs and jokes were sometimes interrupted by the merry laughter or animated conversation of other passengers around us. These nights on the ship were among the pleasant ones of our great journey.

As we arose on the next morning, the slanting rays of the rising sun played on the verdant plains and the receding mountains of the Taurus range. Before us lay the town of Mersina, spreading out on the level shores of Cilicia. We hastened ashore and to the Franciscan church. The fathers here are desperately poor, for the contributions of the natives toward the church are next to nothing, and they have to depend upon the precarious remittances from the Propaganda. Yet they had managed to build a church, though they themselves still lived in a ruinous convent. Our intention was to make an excursion to Tarsus, the reputed birthplace of St. Paul. It lies some twenty miles off to the eastward, in the same wide plain as Mersina. The roads had been paved once upon a time; now the rough huge boulders projected out of the ground, deep ruts had been worn out by the wagon wheels, and bottomless mud-holes yawned for horse and carriage. At a distance of four or five miles to our left, the Taurus, still seamed with streaks of winter's snows, rose over the plain. Waving grain-fields and verdant pastures lined both sides of our road. Bands of men and women, in their wide Turkish garments, were busy here and there cutting the yellow grain with hand-sickles and binding the swelling sheaves as in times of old. I doubt, whether in all this country even one harvesting machine could be found. Why should land-owners invest money in machines, when for a few medjids they could hire hundreds of busy hands? Caravans of heavily laden camels passed us on the road, but also a railroad train rumbled by in the valley to our left. A few Tcherkess horsemen stormed past us like the wind, as we came in sight of Tarsus.

The water of the river Cydnus is skilfully distributed in and around Tarsus by irrigation channels and produces a luxurious vegetation. Trees and shrubs were in full blossom, filling the air with fragrance. We had traversed the lively bazaar streets up and down before we met any one who could understand what we wanted. A young native at last accosted us in English and offered to bring us to the Presbyterian College, and show us the other sights of Tarsus. The Presbyterian College and Seminary are under management of Dr. Christie. When our young guide, who was a student of the seminary, announced us at the home of Dr. Christie, I suppose the good rector had a fainting spell. A Catholic priest paying a visit to the hot-bed of Presbyterian Calvinism in Asia! His wife returned with the message from the

TARSUS

interior (we were not invited to enter, but stood on the doorsteps), that the doctor was not to be seen. They have quite an establishment here, though the buildings would scarcely do for an institution of the same kind in our country. Our young guide seemed somewhat demoralized at the reception which we got. Poor lad, he seemed to think an American Catholic gentleman, and one who seemed just as good as any Protestant minister, ought to be made welcome. Later on, he gave me to understand that he could not account for our reception.

He readily accompanied us to the parish priest of United Armenians. His chapel and dwelling were mere hovels, while the schismatic Armenians near by have a fine church, crowned with a well-proportioned dome. On the outskirts of the town is an immense concrete wall which has withstood the wind and weather of thirty-five centuries. It is said to be the remains of the mausoleum of Sardanapalus. Tarsus is held to be the birthplace of St. Paul by the inhabitants, and they are proud of the distinction. It is at least certain, that he spent a number of years in this town and probably received his education here. The falls of the river Cydnus near the city afford a beautiful bit of natural scenery. Returning to the bazaars, we reveled in the enjoyment of all the dainties of a Turkish dinner. This consisted of nothing more or less than goodly portions of rice pillau and well peppered hash. Only it was supplemented by a bottle of raki. We now knew there was some substantial reason for the huge platters and pots of pillau and meat sauce, that one sees exposed in the open shops of the Turkish towns. Several times afterwards we made hearty meals of these Turkish delicacies.

Our swarthy driver, Gellab, in the meanwhile had fed his horses and now made signs that we must be off on our return, if we would catch the steamer. A few miles out from Tarsus he suddenly jumped off the carriage and ran toward some shepherds in the fields. There he bought a jet black lamb and most unconcernedly placed it between us in the carriage with a bundle of green oats. We were not unwilling to have the gentle beast as our companion and pitied its sad fate, for no doubt it was to serve as food in the near future. One of the industries of this region must be the manufacture of rose-water. A tavern on the roadside was literally hidden from view by the rose-bushes around it and trailing up its sides. The scent of roses filled the air. To the credit of the harbor officials of Mersina be it said, that they, like those of Alexandretta, caused us no delay or trouble in landing or in embarking. The vessel soon had resumed its westerly course along the shores of Cilicia, the moonlit Taurus mountains standing guard to our right. Mrs. Hanson regretted very much that she had not joined us in our excursion to Tarsus, as it had partly been arranged between us the day before. A strong gale blew into the teeth of our vessel, but as she cut straight through the waves, the swaying of the steamer was not considerable and seasickness did not make itself felt.

In the morning, which was Sunday May thirteenth, the great mountain-chain of the Taurus receded to the right and fell into small spurs ahead. Our boat swept northward in a wide curve past the bay of Adalia toward the island of Rhodes. The sea was rough all day and the rebellious play of the waves brought on a sympathetic rebellion of the stomach. But with grim determination I sat on deck, writing about thirty pages of my journal. Frequently the next day we passed islands on both sides of us. Our steamer seemed to have shifted its load, for it hung considerably to the starboard side. Early in the afternoon, the island of Rhodes rose out of the sea and the steamer anchored a few hundred yards from its bastioned harbor-walls. The bright sunlight fell on the old fortifications, now crumbling to ruins on both sides of the lively tree-shaded quay in the centre. Two circular stone piers ran out from each side of the town of Rhodes, ending in two strong towers at a distance of about a hundred yards from each other. The stalwart boatman, as he rowed past between these two towers said that on them stood astride the colossal statue of Rhodes. It must have been an immense statue, if that is true. I suspect that the original towers were much closer together.

How easy these Rhodesians take life! Hundreds of chatting, smoking men in their airy Turkish costumes sat under the trees in full view of the harbor, sipping their coffee from tiny cups and inhaling the fumes of their nargilehs. They eyed us strangers with indolent glances as we passed. None of them seemed to think that the world would stop revolving, if they did not bestir themselves as we Americans do. Our boatman claimed to be a descendant of one of the Spanish knights, who defended Rhodes against the whole Turkish empire for several hundred years. He was only too willing to show us up some of the old streets of the town. The houses evidently were of European origin. Many of them had escutcheons of the noble families on their fronts. But all are falling into ruin. Not a soul is seen on the streets; the men are all down on the shady quay amusing themselves, while the women no doubt are secluded in these old houses.

How easy it was to conjure up the forms of doughty knights of St. John, fighting the Moslem hosts up and down the steep cobbled streets, rivers of blood flowing between the mangled bodies of Christian and Turk to the seashore. Winding through some of the quaint streets, we came up to an old church with armorial bearings of some renowned family over the portals. The church is now used as a mosque. A wide stone stairs and platform leads up to the entrance. Here a band of knights made a desperate stand against the invaders, burying the stairs and platform beneath the bodies of the slain. The boatman pointed to some irregular dark spots on the stones of the stairs, claiming that they are the clots of blood of the slain. But of course that was rather hard to believe.

Our steamer did not weigh anchor until the moon had risen and assumed her sway as the bright queen of the night. We sat in the stern, as the boat turned the bastions and towers of the old fortifications, watching the lights of Rhodes dwindling away, until at last only a solitary red light on a cliff-tower remained on the widening waters. Then the light of the moon grew brighter and brighter, the starry heaven spread its vast arch over the rippling sea and over the distant islands, while the buoyant vessel glided along in the soft zephyrs of the night. These are hours that wake fond musings and often recur to memory in after life.

All forenoon next day, islands continued to rise and sink from our view out of the bosom of the blue deep. About mid-day we passed the island of Samos. The large town, overtopped by a mountain, lay in the sunshine nestled at the water's edge. Samos is almost independent of Turkish dominion, on account of the great number of Greeks that inhabit it. The wine of Samos is famous all over the Orient. Our vessel did not touch at this port, but proceeded to Chios, where we arrived at about two o'clock. We landed with about a dozen gentlemen and a few ladies, and, after strolling through some of the bazaar streets, walked along the fine drive that curves along the beach around the outskirts of the town. Some of the residences, though not very large, were extremely tasteful, for the majority of the 70,000 inhabitants are Greeks, and it appears, well-to-do Greeks. The people seemed somewhat surprised at the large party of strangers invading their town. Many a curious lady's face peeped out behind the venetian blinds, to see what it all meant. The inhabitants are great lovers of flowers. Many had nosegays in their hands or at their breasts; wreaths of flowers decked the doors and windows of the houses; flowers bloomed in the gardens and on the porches of the houses; and the air was laden with perfume. Chios is a good-sized town at the foot of the mountains, that rise a few miles inward. Ruins of the earthquake, which nearly destroyed the town in 1881, still line some of the streets, though most of the town has been rebuilt in modern style.

While sitting in a tavern partaking of some refreshments, a number of Greeks gathered around. I tried to scrape up from the storage rooms of memory, a little of the college Greek. Though the language has not changed so very much, except in some participial constructions, yet the pronunciation of the words is so different from college Greek, that they cannot be recognized. When we returned aboard ship, cattle were being unloaded. Not much ceremony was made with the poor beasts; a chain was placed around their horns in the hold; a signal was given to the man at the steam windlass and up through the hatches they came, held by the horns in mid-air. The derrick was swung over the bulwark and the struggling animal was lowered to a scow below. These cattle being thus disposed of, our steamer cheerily resumed its way to Smyrna. Again we enjoyed the beautiful moonlight, the starry dome of heaven, the calm sea, and the luxury of a reiterated pipe on the stern-deck.

CHAPTER XVII.

In Smyrna — Abusing the Pestering Turk — St. Polycarp's Tomb — The Old Fort on the Mount — In the Streets of Smyrna — Fooling the Dougane — In Marmora Sea — Mytilene and the Dardanelles — Approaching Constantinople — A Fairy View.

We arose early in order to see something of the vast and beautiful bay, at the eastern extremity of which Smyrna is situated. It is the most important city of the Turkish empire next to Constantinople, and contains nearly half a million inhabitants. The sun was just rising and only the smoke of the large city could as yet be seen over the prow of the vessel. High mountains, clothed in the green of olive groves and sloping pastures, lined the shore to our right. Two peaks called the "Two Brothers," or "Les Mamelles" overtopped all the rest. Two towns in the midst of gardens and varying fields were nestled halfway up their sloping bases. Farther on the large buildings of a fashionable bathing resort lay half concealed in a mountain gorge. The shores of the bay to our left were low and seemed to be more adapted to commercial and manufacturing pursuits. A great deal of salt for the government monopoly is obtained on the sand-beach

The first object that is apt to catch the eye on approaching Smyrna is the great fort, dating from the time when the Genoese had possession. It occupies the brow of the mountain behind Smyrna. The city is spread out below along the sloping banks. Half way up the hill a vast, dark area of cypress trees divided into two portions indicates the Turkish cemetery. Every Mussulman likes to be buried, if possible, beneath the dark green roof of the stately cypress.

Our steamer dropped anchor amid the numerous other vessels, close in-shore. A host of boatmen surrounded the vessel in order to bring the passengers to the custom house only a hundred feet away. A swarthy Greek captured us two, and agreed to land us and bring us back to the ship for a stipulated price. Our good opinion of Turkish harbor officials that had gradually grown upon us, was doomed to rude destruction. Our passes had seemed in perfect order to all those whom we had so far encountered in the smaller harbors; now they were closely scrutinized and we were detained. Mine, the superintendent said, had not been viséed in Jaffa and must now be signed by government officials here. My companion's had not been viséed since leaving America, and was entirely worthless. Both could be set in order only by getting the signature of identification from the American consul. I would have to pay three, my companion eight medjid, before we could be allowed to enter Smyrna.

I wonder to this day that the superintendent of the custom police did not arrest us on the spot for the lively row that now ensued between us and him. I know that any policeman in the United States would not have taken half the abuse the Turkish government got that day. I was thoroughly incensed at the unreasonableness of the demands. However, the Smyrnians seem to allow Americans a pretty wide berth in the kicking line. It was not so long ago that two American cruisers had entered this port to bombard the city, if a certain indemnity was not immediately forthcoming. Our guide afterwards told us that the indemnity was paid, but that the business people would have liked to see the American tars stay longer. Business had taken a boom during their presence. Our protests were not without result, for the superintendent finally allowed us to land on giving guarantees that we would procure the necessary signatures during the day.

The streets near the water are lined with great business houses, that is, great for the country we were in. Nothing of course like those of large American or European cities. A mule tramway runs along the main street and terminates near the extensive barracks and military grounds. Bordering the latter is the busiest portion of the city, and the great hall of justice. The open porticos on the ground floor of the palace of justice were swarming with people and the fragrance of beautiful flower-gardens which extend on one side of the building, wafted in through the hallways. While our dragoman attended to the necessary formalities connected with the renewal of our passes, we sat in one of the Turkish coffee-houses opposite. There they sat, the ease-loving Turks, in their loose garments, some in lively conversation over their strong coffee, others filling their lungs with the smoke of costly nargilehs. The Turkish expression for smoking is "to drink the smoke" and very much like drinking their mode of inhaling seems to be. They do not take short puffs, but they inhale the smoke into their lungs as we would inhale the air in a long breath. On little tables tiny cups of coffee, or glasses of the milky raki, or some other more cooling drink is served. In Rome do as the Romans, so I ordered one of the water-pipes and the other good things. The waiter, it seemed, wanted to please me, for he brought the finest nargileh in the establishment. The thick amber mouthpiece was at least six inches long, studded with jewels and inlaid with silver. The same adornments were on the long hose and on the joints at the crystal bowl. He heaped up uncut tobacco leaves on the silver top and applied fire. But I succeeded but indifferently in keeping the tobacco lighted. In the short time at my disposal I failed to see the luxury of holding the thick mouth-piece in the mouth and drawing away at it like an asthmatic. Beggars and peddlers of all kinds made their rounds, but every now and then the managers would rudely drive them out. Most of the beggars, our guide told us, were from Crete, where the Greeks are much oppressed by their Turkish masters since the last troubles of the Turkish empire with Greece.

As our guide had returned with the required passes it was time to be astir. Our first objective point was the old Genoese fort on th hill. Along the winding road up the hill were the extensive barracks and parade grounds, where Turkish soldiers were drilling. We met several guards on the road who scrutinized the passengers for contraband goods, especially tobacco. From the top of the crumbling fortifications on the summit of the hill there is a magnificent view of the widespreading city below, of the blue bay and the shores beyond, and of the verdant valleys and wooded mountains toward the in-terior. The fort itself is but a ruin. The cement of the wall is so durable that it still holds together in huge blocks. In the center are large excavations, which were used as underground store-rooms by the garrison. A tunneled passage is said to run ten miles underground to the site of ancient Ephesus.

We picked our way down the mountain to a place where a small building like a monument had attracted our attention. A green flag floated from it, as also from several other places. They indicate the burying places of Mohammedan dervishes or persons considered saints by the Mohammedans. This particular monument is venerated by the Mohammedans as the burying-place of St. Polycarp, the disciple of St. John. It was hard to figure out what connection these Turks could have with St. Polycarp. He was martyred here about five hundred years before their preposterous Mahomet was born. Why should they set up a monument on a spot where he probably never was buried, and claim it as a holy place? But if they really believed it to be his resting-place, why should they parade a whitewashed, crumbling wall as a befitting monument for so great a saint? On certain days the Moslems gather here and offer sacrifice of sheep, which is another curious anomaly, certainly not warranted by the Koran. That the keeper was not deceiving us in this regard, was evidenced by the fact that the trees behind the low structure were bespattered with clotted blood.

After indulging in a regular Turkish dinner, in which pillau of course figured prominently, we strolled through the rich bazaars of the city. The silk and embroidery are especially remarkable in these bazaars. They are covered by glass roofs. Several caravans of camels passed through the narrow passages, while we sauntered through. The best way to avoid a collision with the heavily laden beasts is to duck under their widespreading loads, for you must not expect a camel, no more than a solid wall, to yield an inch. Get out of the way, or it will walk over you.

We visited the Catholic church of St. Polycarp in the heart of the city. The front half of the church and many of the marble ornaments date back to the fourth century. It has lately been enlarged, so that now it contains three naves, most beautifully decorated. The style of the interior is a peculiarly pleasing mixture of the Renaissance and Byzantine. One of the fathers in charge of the parish disbelieved any connection between the Moslem tomb and St. Polycarp, except that a very unreliable tradition indicated that neighborhood as the place of his martyrdom.

On getting aboard again, I found that I had lost one of the books that I had bought. Not wishing to have any more trouble with the boats, I climbed onto a scow which connected with the shore. This mode of getting ashore was altogether against the regulations of the custom house, but none of the guards noticed me. The trouble came when I returned the same way. Just as I reached the ship's ladder, guards came rushing along the shore shouting after me. As quickly as possible I mounted over the bulwarks out of their sight. I knew that they could not have gotten a full view of me in their excitement. Therefore I deliberately carried a steamer chair to the sterndeck and sat myself down, looking at them as if their shouting and running were only a matter of complacent curiosity to me. One of them ventured to point me out to the rest, but as I seemed only highly amused, he began to doubt my identity. For about fifteen minutes the guards searched the vessel, while I sat in full view. They finally gave up the search. This was at least some satisfaction for the trouble they had caused me in the morning.

A certain doctor in Smyrna had alarmed the city by claiming that he had found a case of bubonic plague. But as the statement proved false, the wrath of the inhabitants was thoroughly roused. They gathered at his residence, and would have mobbed him if the police had not made it possible for him to escape from the city. Only a few days later, however, the plague did really break out, and quarantine was enforced against all vessels that touched there after us. At about seven o'clock the Aphrodite steamed out of the spacious bay and headed northward to the Dardanelles.

In the morning the loud voice of the captain roused us from sleep in order to undergo examination by the doctor. He had come aboard from Mytilene, where our vessel lay anchored. The city was soon spread out on the sloping shores on both sides of a headland. An old fort occupied the summit of a hill, the dark walls of which straggled up and down over the declivities. At one o'clock we passed the island of Tenedos, of Homeric renown, and soon after the plateau-lands of old Ilion, or Troy. Then the narrow passage of the Dardanelles hove in sight. The shores of the ocean approach each side for two or three miles like the banks of a river, though in other places they again recede to form wide basins.

In the harbor of Renku, just before entering the sea of Marmora or Hellespont, we were detained several hours by custom officers. English steamers and tugs disported themselves in the blue waters and the dazzling rays of the sun were reflected from the intensely white buildings of Renku. The vessel proceeded very slowly, for on the next morning we were still in the sea of Marmora. The lead-colored waters of Marmora stretched away to the dim and hazy shores on both sides, until San Stefano and Makriki appeared on the low banks to the left. These towns are only some eighteen miles from Constantinople. The Russian army had advanced to this neighborhood in the last Turkish war of 1878, when England and the other powers interfered to save the Sick Man of the East. To the right of us the islands of Pinte, Antigone, Chalkis, and Principe, famous pleasure resorts for the inhabitants of Constantinople, rose out of the sea. Behind them the Asiatic Olympus gleamed in perpetual snows.

On entering the Bosphorus we were of course on the lookout for the first view of Constantinople. All travelers agree that the view of the city from the entrance of the Bosphorus is one of the most beautiful sights to be seen anywhere. Unfortunately the atmosphere was filled with haziness and the heavens were covered with rain-clouds; on this account we lost much of the beauty of the scene. Yet even so the view was beautiful. As the ship rounded the four islands, the city began to rise over the waters like a fairy creation. The countless towers and minarets, St. Sophia and the old palaces of Stambul; then the branch waters of the Bosphorus, and the Golden Horn passed in view. Soon also appeared the tower of Galata, and back of it the buildings of Pera overlooking the Golden Horn and the older Istambul. As the vessel skimmed along the narrowing channel of the Bosphorus, both these divisions of the city unfolded themselves more and more, while to the right the green heights of Bulgourlu and the suburbs on the Asiatic shore glided into view. Farther on some of the great white palaces and old castles line both sides of the magnificent Bosphorus. The distant mountains cut off the view of the Black sea.

CHAPTER XVIII.

Custom House Amenities — Dancing Dervishes —
On the Golden Horn — Perversity in Gray
Hairs — Turkish Harems Turned Loose —
Rainbound — Galata and Pera — The Ubiqui-
tous Dog — Nocturnal Harmony.

Our ship dropped anchor opposite Galata, the
Genoese addition to Stambul. A host of small boats
soon encircled the vessel to wait for passengers. Most
of them had followed us for an hour or more. Naturally
we were anxious to get ashore. But we were in Turkish
territory, where time seems to be of no value. We
waited several hours for the laggard doctors in order to
undergo the insignificant examination for quarantine.
It was long past noon when we were finally permitted
to consign ourselves to the tender mercies of the ravenous
boatmen, runners, and custom officials. The latter
marauders, failing to see us offer a sufficient bakshish,
retained the fragment of a Greek bible and some
Baedeckers from our baggage. They gave us to understand that these books must be examined lest they contain
anything derogatory to the Turkish government. We
took our lodgings at Hotel Kroeker on Pera Hill, whence
we had a splendid view of old Stambul from our third-
story window.

At dinner a gray-haired man, who had just arrived
from Bohemia, was volubly talking to any and every
one, evidently considering himself a man who had seen
something of the world and was entitled to be heard.
In our presence he unspun all his plans for his three
weeks' stay to Philips, our guide. "The first thing we

must do to-day," he said, "is to make the trip up the Golden Horn," for on Friday (which it happened to be that day) all the beauties of the harems would be gathered on its banks. Philips had already made engagements to that effect with him. However, as the dancing dervishes were to have their weekly performance in a mosque not far off, we left the eccentric Bohemian to his own volubility for the present and betook ourselves to that place.

It was an octagonal building, the center of which was portioned off by a circular railing as a dancing floor. Already the other space between the walls and railing was filled with spectators. At the head of the dancing floor there was an opening in the railing, behind which some distinguished Turks in rich uniforms were sitting. Along the circular railing on the dancing floor, in groups of three and with bowed heads, sat the dervishes. They wore gray caps, something like stovepipes without rims, and were dressed in plaited petticoats. From the gallery were heard the muffled sounds of kettle-drums and squeaking instruments. Presently these sounds were augmented by a howling song. Thereupon the dervishes began to raise their heads as if awakened from a trance. They got on their feet and began to walk around, making a low bow whenever they passed a green-mantled Turk, at the opening of the railing. After the second round they began to whirl around like tops, using one foot as a pivot. Faster and faster they whirled, more and more unearthly screeched and rumbled the music above. The dervishes began to stretch out their arms, holding one palm upward, the other downward, head and eyes turned heavenward. Their loose gowns began to spread out centrifugally, so that they looked like weird witches in immense hoopskirts. The din above was now and then interrupted by a loud wail, while the green-mantled overseer cast an eye of disapproval on the laggards to urge them to greater celerity. So these bony, fantastic forms, some young, some old, kept whirling around on their one foot and moving around the circle for half an hour.

It seemed most senseless to the beholder. They, however, imagine that they are engaged in the highest kind of prayer, and in a total abandonment in the hands of Allah. But as far as outward appearance is concerned, it would be hard to find more repulsive features on the streets of Constantinople. We left before they had ceased their whirling, in order to make our excursion to the sweet waters of Europe, or the Golden Horn

Worshek, the Bohemian, meanwhile had gotten himself ready, and we soon arrived at the old bridge and installed ourselves in one of the river-ferries. They ply in all directions and serve as the principal means of communication between the different parts of the city. Our gray-haired companion drew upon himself the attention of the motley crowds on the steamer by his loud and conceited remarks. He was a regular coxcomb in spite of his gray hair, babbling about the charms of the women around him and wishing they would only raise their veils. When I used the word "harem," he warned me not to use that word again. If any Turks would hear that word, we would certainly be mobbed. The old man remembered having read this in some antediluvian guidebook. Of course we could but laugh at the vain fears of our lively companion.

Having swiftly passed up the Golden Horn between old Stambul on the left and Pera on the right, we disembarked in order to make the rest of the way in one of the graceful boats which can be rented on the banks. They are manned by dexterous oarsmen. The Golden Horn soon narrows to a medium-sized stream, for it is nothing else than a brook, which comes down from the mountains on the European side, and which has been widened out to a distance of about three miles from Constantinople. Its banks have been turned into gardens and pleasant lawns for public pleasure-grounds. At the foot of the hills there are some villages belonging to the Sultan's family. Thousands of boats, gaily decorated, some large, others small, swarmed in the narrowing channel.

Along the banks were men and women of all ages and conditions, in all sorts of dress. The Turkish women, either by themselves or accompanied by the men, moved about or sat on the grass or under leafy bowers. Nearly all wore veils, occasionally drawn up and allowing glimpses of their features, they themselves casting sly looks at the passers-by. Our old Bohemian hotspur stared at the women, calling them beauties and making other loud remarks about them. I myself could see nothing particularly charming about their depressed and pale faces. They looked to me more like despairing invalids, out for a breath of fresh air. The women of Europe and America do not know what a sad life four-fifths of their sex live in heathen and Mohammedan countries. They are the mere toys or slaves of the brutalized men. In Christian countries woman is regarded as the equal, and in some respects, as the superior of man, as long as she knows how to keep her place. Through the Mother of Christ she has been raised from her position of slavery, to the level of man. Through Her alone she has regained some of the charms of the original Eve, whereby she reigns over the heart of the sterner sex. The "new woman" is on a fair way to return to the position of her sisters in the Orient.

When we had rowed up the Golden Horn about half the distance, rain seemed imminent and most of the countless boats were pushing homeward. Among them were also some large barges, with fifty or sixty persons, who had rowed up from the Black Sea. On one of these a negro was dancing and singing for the amusement of the crowd. At the end of the Sweet Waters we alighted and took some lemonade in a summerhouse built of leafy branches of trees. Several carriages passed us with members of the Sultan's household. On our return it began to rain, but there was still a great number of boats with merry passengers. The Turkish soldiers and officers made themselves especially noticeable, as is soldier fashion all over Europe when ladies are present. The shower did not last long and behind us the sun again broke through the rain-clouds. As we approached Stambul and Pera the bright yellow light of the evening flashed from the windows of the old palaces and buildings on the terraced hillside, and made the city seem a world of fire.

Old Worshek had kept up his incessant babbling and now took me to task, because I had said I would not be ready for a start in the morning, until I had transacted my business at a certain church. This started him off on religion, and he asked me, whether I was still so benighted as to believe in the existence of a God. Nowadays, he said, not one in a hundred persons could be found in Europe, that still believed in a personal God. Of course we all laughed heartily at the absurdity of his assertion. We had just come from Jerusalem, where five hundred of his countrymen had made the pilgrimage to the grave of the Godman. I asked him how it came, that he himself was continually using the name of God in his conversation. "O, that is only a habit," he said. His brother, he said, was one of those fools, that still practice the religion which his parents had instilled into them in their youth; he himself was more enlightened. Philips, the guide, and even the Turkish boatman when he came to understand what our conversation was about, could not repress their disgust at the vagaries of the gray-haired infidel. He was getting quite angry, for he saw that none of his arguments had a ghost of a show in the company, and that he was making a laughing-stock of himself. Rising up in the boat and clenching his fist toward heaven, he defied the Almighty to strike him dead, and he gave me leave to call down upon him the thunderbolts of heaven. I asked him whether his excitement was not a new proof, that in his heart he believed in the existence of a God, and whether it was not evidently a vain attempt to suppress the secret dread of an outraged deity in his heart? Perhaps before he would get back to Bohemia, he would find out how well grounded his fears were. It was certainly a disgusting sight to see an old man disporting himself in such a manner.

From some remark that I made after we had landed, he learnt that I was one of the "brood of Catholic priests," as he called them on the boat. He was quite taken aback, when he saw that he had been talking to a Catholic priest all the while, and it seemed he was somewhat ashamed of himself. I told him to be at ease, for I had met people of his stamp before, and I knew how to condole with them. The poor man had very likely associated only with the ignorant riff-raff of humanity, that tries to conceal their inward dread of punishment by their malicious ranting against the existence of God. This time at least he had met some one ready to contradict his blasphemies with a violence equal to his own, and found that his arguments brought him nothing but ridicule. At supper the insuppressible old man monopolized the conversation of the whole dining-room, and, having bluffed the rest of the party into silence, he addressed himself to me across the table. He made some slighting remarks concerning the United States. I asked him on what authority he made the statements, he answered that he had "heard it said." I asked him pointedly, whether he knew nothing about that country, except what "was said," which made him subside like the froth on the tip of a wave. He steered shy of me during the rest of our stay at hotel Kroeker.

The next day was the first really rainy day which we experienced on our trip since we left Manila. The streets were not in a fit condition to do much sight-seeing. We managed, however, to find the nearest Catholic church, that of St. Anthony, in charge of the Italian Franciscans. Rev. Othmar Blanchard, a Swiss father, treated us very kindly. In the afternoon during a pause in the rain we strolled along the main street running up from Galata through Pera. It presents an appearance quite European, fine stores and other buildings lining it on both sides. But it is a very narrow part of the way and the sidewalks are mostly stone paths, not by far wide enough for the great number of passengers. It is traversed by narrow and rickety horse-cars, on which the charges are in inverse proportion to the convenience afforded. My criticisms in that regard were listened to with evident satisfaction by the passengers who rode down to Galata with us; yet they seemed cautious in their answers. I afterwards found out, that it is not at all safe for anyone to criticise under the rule of Abdul Hamid, especially not for any of the inhabitants. I often noticed, that they eyed me with suspicion and cast cautious glances around on the by-standers, when I launched out in criticism. No one is sure, whether government spies are not hovering around to catch a treasonous word in order to bring it to headquarters.

Leaving the cars near the Galata strand, we strolled up and down some of the busiest streets. This part of Constantinople dates back to the time of the Genoese in the thirteenth century. When the Moslems took Stambul from them, the Genoese were allowed to settle outside the old walls across the Golden Horn. Quite a number of Christians gathered here in course of time, and they built a tower on the summit of the hill for purposes of defense. This tower is now used for a watch-tower of the fire department. Between this tower and the shores of the Bosphorus are many ruinous and narrow lanes, some of them having no outlet. Here the sailors and beggars and the more villainous portion of the population have their haunts and pursue their secret or boisterous vocations and carousals. It is no doubt an unsavory neighborhood for the stranger, and it is not provided with any superfluous illumination. There were numerous resorts for pleasure or for drink in the by-ways and lanes, all well frequented. Nearer to the water and towards the bridge, the streets are crowded with people of all nations and all conditions, from the ragged Turk or Kurd hamal to the rich merchant with gaudy turban or red fez and wide pantaloons; the swarthy Arab or armed Cherkese mingles with the swell Armenian or sight-hunting European traveler.

Of course we soon became acquainted with the real street-owners of Constantinople. They enjoy great privileges without paying any taxes. Theirs is the right of way, respected even by the street-car monopoly. Besides, they have a first lien on all perquisites for sustaining life, that may be found on the streets. I refer to the dogs of Constantinople: a wolfish, longtailed, blear-eyed progeny, covered with dirty gray or brownish bristling hair and occupying, singly or in packs, the walks, the gutters, and cobble-pavements of the streets. No genuine native of the city would think of disturbing the beasts as they lie in his way. Much less would any of these four-legged lords of the streets make an offer to get up for any biped, man or woman, that might have occasion to use the path. Carts or carriages must make a detour for their litters lying in the middle of the street. Each neighborhood is in possession of a certain breed of dogs, who will quickly tear to pieces any dog from another quarter, that may stray among them. Not unfrequently a dozen curs could be seen scouring across a square furiously pursuing a luckless canine, whom hunger or love-making had induced to leave the territory in which he first saw the light of day. Now and then a loud snarling resounded, where a group of dogs of the same territory fell to quarreling over some castaway bone or other garbage. They are the scavengers of Constantinople, which in a measure might explain the privileges they enjoy. As it had rained on this day, they had assumed special rights over any dry spot on the pavement or narrow walks. The foot-passengers therefore were not unfrequently obliged to step into the mud of the gutter in order to pass around the festive canines. One of them had installed herself with a litter of some nine half-blind pups in a box on the middle of the walk. Another was fondly licking a couple of her progeny on the stone sill of a palatial building. No one thought of driving them out of the way, and some of them snarled viciously at passengers who dared to come too near in passing.

Our objective point had been the douane or custom-house, where we wanted to make inquiries about the books which had been detained the day before. For some time we were unable to find an outlet in the maze of streets of Galata, but when we finally reached the douane, they told us that our books had not yet been examined and we must wait. It had in the meanwhile begun to grow dusk and to rain, so our walk up the hill was not of the pleasantest. However, we reached hotel Kroeker without sustaining any other harm than the rain could do us. This we soon forgot at the supper-table and in our room upstairs.

The rain kept up its incessant splash on the sill of the open window during the night. Adjoining the hotel were the remains of a large cypress grove, which formerly served as a Mohammedan cemetery. Streets had been cut through it, many of the trees had disappeared, and business houses had invaded the abode of the dead. On some other night, as we sat at the open window, the wonderful harmony of a song reached our ears. It came from a party of Greeks, who were passing through this cemetery. Faintly at first from the distance the four-voiced song trembled through the night air, then louder and louder as they approached, dying away again, as they passed down toward the water. Very often during the night, peculiarly sharp thuds sounded up from the streets. The night-watchmen thump the pavement with their ironclad staffs as they make their rounds. A fine arrangement for the thieves and crooks: they could calculate to a minute, how long they might continue in any incident night-job, before the watchman would be close enough to interfere. What matters a small intermission? The receding thumps of the staff would soon indicate the peaceful passage of the watchman, and they could resume their work. I think our policemen could learn a trick or two from these night-watchmen in Constantinople; they could learn to make their rounds in dangerous places without fear of encountering any member of the fraternity of night-workers.

CHAPTER XIX.

Mass in Istambul — Over the Swarming Bridge
— Agia Sophia — Old Remnants — Stambul
Scenes — To Skutari — Splendid View —
About Armenian Massacres — On Horseback
over the Hills — Sunset on the Bosphorus —
Black and Roaring Waters — Much Ado about
Nothing — Over Ruined Walls.

I had been invited by Father Blanchard to say mass
at eight o'clock on Sunday. It is the glorious privilege
of the Catholic traveler to be able to attend the same
kind of worship that he has been accustomed to since
his childhood, in all parts of the world, though he may
be ten thousand miles from home. He begins to understand, that he belongs truly to the one universal and
unchangeable church, unchangeable by time or place.
In the midst of Mohammedanism we could kneel and
join in the same glorious homage of the Savior and in the
same consoling veneration of the Queen of Heaven.
Here and in many French and Italian churches I saw
some men of the congregation during service kneeling
and receiving Holy Communion in the sanctuary, while
the women received it at the communion railing.

Generally there are very few seats in European
churches; the congregation kneel or stand promiscu-
ously on the stone pavement. On examining the reg-
ister of the Sacristy I found the name of Rev. Heuser,
editor of the Ecclesiastical Review, and also the names
of the priests of the German caravan to Jerusalem.

After breakfast we went to get a good view of Constantinople from the Galata tower. A circular stairs

leads round the massive walls to the height of about fifty meters. Six centuries of wear have hollowed out the two hundred steps that lead to the top. From its tin-covered roof we could survey the whole surrounding: St. Sophia and the other great mosques, the arches of the ancient aqueduct more than a thousand years old, the remains of the city walls, winding around the old city from the Golden Horn to the Sea of Marmora. The obelisk, dating back to Roman times, and the Seraskian tower overtop the sea of buildings in the middle of old Stambul. To the south, across the Bosphorus, Skutari, Bulgourlu hill, and several other suburbs lined the shore, while the Asiatic Olympus gleamed over the Princess islands. The morning sun had driven off the rain-clouds of the previous day and brightly shone over all the varied panorama.

The old bridge, connecting Galata with Stambul, is only a ramshackle wooden affair resting on pontoons, but it is a goldmine for the Sultan. They do not bother the passengers with tickets; six or seven collectors on each end stand in a row across the roadway collecting the metaliques from the crowds as they pass. You pay your cash and pass over or stay on the bridge all day, if you like. It is quite worth while lingering, for there is probably no place in the world, where so many and so varied kinds of people pass within a given time, as on this bridge. What a vast variety of physiognomies even in one hour! It seems as if all the nations of the world had appointed this their meeting-place on the confines of Europe and Asia.

Omitting a visit to the mausoleum Valide at the other end of the bridge, we entered on the Serai or old palace grounds of Constantinople. The palaces are mostly in ruins, but the grounds are laid out in drives and patches of park. A plantain tree, dating back to remote times, measures thirty-five feet in circumference at a man's height. Under it, in times gone by, many a squad of Janizaries have lain, opposite the gate of death, where their clamor for the heads of obnoxious pashas rose up to the windows of the Sultan's palace. And here they dispatched many a victim of their resentment as soon as the Sultan had yielded to their clamors and sent them their victims through the old portals of the Serai. Passing under this gate of death, we stood in sight of the great mosque St. Sophia. Exteriorly it looks like a conglomeration of smaller buildings and additions surmounted by a vast cupola. During the Moslem occupation additions have been made to the great church without any regard for taste or architecture, so that any architectural beauty of the outside, if there was any originally, is completely hidden. Justinian, who completed it, would scarcely recognize it, if he were to come upon it of a sudden.

Passing by the main portal, which is reserved solely for the Sultan, we came through a narrow street to the front, where a vast carved door gave entrance to an arched hall or atrium. From this hall several entrances open into the main body of the mosque. The Turks will not neglect this chance of collecting bakshish from the stranger. Any giaour, that wants to inspect the mosque, must pay a medjid, equal to one dollar. The corridor or vestibule is richly decorated with mosaics and the great doors are of carved bronze. Before entering the mosque proper a Turk will intercept you and require you to put on slippers or take off your shoes. Inside, the vast dome rises magnificently on four marble columns. These columns are spanned by four immense arches which support the lower base of the cupola. So correct is the proportion that at first one does not realize the dimensions of the great dome. The substructure, above which this vast cupola rises, is the form of a cross and about 270 feet wide. A gallery 50 feet wide runs around three sides behind the marble pillars, which support the dome. The whole vast surface of the dome and of the walls down to a certain height, was formerly of rich mosaics, but now is daubed with tasteless stencil arabesques in yellow, black, or blue colors. In many of the fields the mosaic images of the saints and of the Savior, that adorned the church in Christian times, still appear in outline behind the Moslem daubing.

The whole area of the mosque is bare of furniture except the mihrab and two huge wax candlesticks. Around some of the pillars were railings, within which dervishes were reciting the Koran in loud monotonous voices. One little chap was all alone within one of these railings, swinging to and fro on his knees in his efforts to get the Koran by heart. To the left of the mihrab, a black stone slab was immured into the wall: this is a piece of the Kaaba at Mecca and is held most sacred by the Moslems. Many pious Turks make pilgrimages to this stone instead of going to Mecca. Under the galleries are spacious porticos or halls, supported by pillars of rare stone. The larger of these pillars, supporting the principal arches of the halls, are spoils from renowned buildings of ancient times. The vaulted ceilings of the porticos are beautifully mosaicked.

Though the Agia Sophia was founded by Constantine, Justinian, two hundred years later, is its rebuilder and completer. It is therefore nearly fourteen hundred years old. In 1452 it passed into the hands of the Mohammedans. On one of the great columns near the western entrance, at a height of about fifteen feet, is seen a daub of red color. The Turks believe that it is the impress of the hand of Mahomet II on the day of his victorious entrance. The last refuge of the defenders of the city was St. Sophia. Around this pillar were piled the bodies of the slain ten feet high. When all the Christians had been slain, Mahomet climbed on top of this heap of

ST. SOPHIA

dead and laid his gory hand against this pillar in sign of victory. No amount of paint, according to Moslem belief, will wipe out this stain. St. Sophia did not strike me as the great wonder it is claimed to be. The dome of St. Peter in Rome is 193 feet in diameter and 448 feet high, while that of St. Sophia is only 107 feet across and 183 high. Of course the fact, that the Turks have so miserably disfigured the interior by their daubing, and the fact, that the building is misused for a mosque rather than for its original purpose as a Christian church, must be taken into consideration.

Not far from Agia Sophia is the ancient hippodrome, or rather the remains of it; namely, the bronze serpentine pillar, broken at half its length, the carved obelisk, and traces of the race course. Many a gay scene, no doubt, was here witnessed in the times of the Roman emperors of the East. Nearby is the Janizar museum, containing life-size wax figures of army and court officials, dressed in the uniforms used during the centuries of Turkish domination. The Ahmet mosque is an imitation of St. Sophia, with a larger dome. Its interior is covered with white and blue tile, making it look still more bare and cold than that of St. Sophia. Of the many mausoleums of Constantinople, that of Hamid Assis is the most remarkable. The members of the Sultan's family are here buried under sarcophagi, covered with black velvet palls, richly embroidered. Costly memorials from the sovereigns of Europe are placed around in the same apartment, among them two heavy candlesticks from Queen Victoria, and a magnificent golden clock from the emperor of France. On silver stands are copies of the Koran written by the Sultans; that of Haroun al Rashid being especially remarkable. Each Sultan is expected to copy the Koran at least once in his life. In the beautiful cemetery surrounding the mosque are the monuments of the many celebrated Turkish statesmen and generals of former times. The whole cemetery seemed one bouquet of exquisite flowers, especially roses in full bloom.

A few turns brought us into the midst of the old streets and lanes of Stambul. In one of the small lunch rooms we had a dinner in regular Turkish fashion. These dinners, as I have remarked before, are admirably adapted to drive away hunger and not merely to pass away time. Our good dragoman, Philips, did not forget himself in giving orders, you may be sure. Afterwards he persuaded us to go to the bazaars, where he expected his friends, the stall-keepers, to ease us of some of our superfluous cash. This time it was in the shape of rosewater, which we had hinted as a possible purchase. The native merchant brought out six glass sticks bored like a thermometer, each containing about a drop and a half of the fluid and offered them to us at forty francs. He said that was about their price in any other shop. With great perversity we offered ten or twelve francs and finally concluded the bargain at twenty francs. With much ado, the Turk asked us whether we would take it on our conscience to make him lose so much at one fell swoop. We though we could take that and much more on our conscience. Afterwards we found out that to have offered five francs would have been a very liberal offer for the stuff.

All kinds of European and Oriental merchandise is exposed under these glass-covered roofs of the vast bazaars. A goodly proportion of the merchandise sold as Oriental is made in wholesale quantities in Europe and America and shipped to the Orient. The shop-keepers are of course always on the alert for the stranger and mostly succeed in palming off their goods at fancy prices. The guide generally extols the wares to the skies and gets a share of the booty. On the whole, the bazaars pleased me less than those I had seen in the far East.

Under the glass roofs they have lost much of the Oriental variety and picturesqueness, and I fancy, that in a few years they will resemble merely our great department stores.

Our next move was a passage on one of the steamboats across the Bosphorus to Skutari. There we soon procured three fine horses for a ride up to the heights of Bulgourlu. Skutari is a large addition to Constantinople on the Asiatic side of the Bosphorus. The streets here are wide and the houses seem commodious. The road up to Bulgourlu leads through some of these streets and then past fine gardens, residences, and summer-resorts on the slopes of the hill. Our horses, though hired, had some fire of youth left, and each one of us, as is usual with those seldom on horseback, thought it his duty to show a little of his horsemanship. So, every now and then, one or the other of us would whip up the horse he was riding and make a spurt; of course the other two would have to follow, if they did not want to load upon themselves eternal shame as indifferent riders. My traveling companion claimed, that he often hired horses in Dubuque on Sunday afternoons to ride out with his friends. I of course, as a Bedouin sheik, and one that had done a great deal of camping out, had to keep up some sort of appearances. As for our guide Philips, he had to prove himself a good rider on general principles, for these guides claim to be paragons of all kinds of acquisition and skill. To tell the truth, however, the three of us must have been shamming; in our inmost souls we were conscious of the insecurity of our exalted position, and after a while, no doubt, also of the chafing and thumping of certain portions of our anatomy, used to more sedate and gentle treatment. But what will vanity not accomplish?

We arrived on the top of the mount in less than an hour, and were rewarded by a charming prospect and a pleasant rest on the greensward. Other pleasure seekers were scattered here and there on the hilltop; some well to do Armenians, some Greeks and Turks. An awning was put up by some enterprising individual, under which he sold lemonade and other refreshments. Pieces of Turkish Delight, a sort of soft candy steeped in powdered sugar, were brought with each order. Constantinople, spread out in the sunshine on the other shore of the Bosphorus, lined with beautiful villas and summer resorts, stretched away to our right where the opening of the Bosphorus permitted a glimpse of the Black sea through dark mountain walls. Glassy Marmora stretched away to our left, varied by the group of islands on the horizon. Behind us the verdant hills and valleys of Asiatic Turkey met the gaze in glorious sunshine. On looking from this mountain over these pleasant scenes, one is loth to remember, that this beautiful country was wrested from Christian civilization by the barbaric Turk, and that his blighting footstep still rests on these fair provinces. Tyranny and bloodshed terrorize the inhabitants. Philips, casting a wary glance at the pleasure seekers, that might be within hearing, said that he himself had witnessed the stabbing, shooting, and cudgeling of inhabitants in the streets of Constantinople three years ago. According to his assertions, the Armenians were really the first aggressors, throwing stones and shooting from housetops at Turkish soldiers, in the hope of causing an insurrection against the Sultan's government. Thereupon the Turkish soldiers began to massacre every Armenian found walking the streets of Constantinople, and they were seconded in a lively manner by the Turkish populace.

Again we bestrode our horses and descended in a different direction toward the great Moslem cemetery on the Asiatic side. It is seen as a vast cypress forest on the slope of the hill. The devout Mussulman does not like to rest on European soil, but will seek to be buried on Asiatic soil, where the tomb of Mahomet and the Kaaba stands. This accounts for the vastness of this cemetery. The high cypress trees are so closely planted, that their crowns completely shut out the light of day. Even more thickly beneath them are set the upright slabs of stone, that mark the graves of the Moslems. Some of the stones are left in their natural roughness as they come from the quarry, others have a turbaned head carved on top. Many of them are standing upright, others are beginning to topple over or are lying pell-mell on the ground in great confusion. As much as the Moslem likes to visit his graveyards and cherish the memory of the dead, he cares little to exert himself in propping up the falling headpieces or repair the ravages of time. If the headstone falls, is it not the will of Allah? Through the midst of this grove we rode on a water-washed trail, the stones looking like the heads of ghosts on the wayside. In many places the path led over groups of these fallen stones. Robbers are said to infest this cemetery, for in the vast recesses of its forest they would find thousands of hiding places to elude any pursuit. So deep is the shade cast by the trees, that a perpetual gloom reigns beneath, and though it was a hot sunny day, the air was quite chilly.

Issuing again from these dismal scenes into the sunlight, Philips set his horse into a gallop over a wide pasture; we followed of course, neck or nothing, over the uneven ground. As mine seemed to be the best of the three nags, it soon overtook Philip's, while the third spurted on behind. We rode past the English church and graveyard where the soldiers who fell in the Crimean war are buried. In the summer-resort nearby a band of Bohemian girls gave a concert, while the garden in front was filled with listening and ogling men.

Instead of one of the large ferries, which we missed, we

took a rowboat to cross the broad Bosphorus. Swiftly the sharp bow cleaved the waves, as the last rays of the sun glittered on the water and fringed the storm-clouds above the city with burnished gold. Before we had half crossed, the dusk began to settle. But by the lusty exertions of the two oarsmen we reached the old bridge and elbowed our way through the throngs to our hotels. We had put in a busy day of sight-seeing, and when we counted up our expenses, we found that they amounted to about 220 piastres for both, which would make nearly nine dollars of American money. But this expense was quite unusual with us; all our expenses, including railroad and steamer tickets for the journey, amounted on an average to only seven dollars a day. Conservative travelers estimate the daily expense of a journey at about eight dollars a person, not counting the amount spent for transportation.

After mass at St. Anthony's next day we took passage in one of the steamers up the Bosphorus nearly to the Black sea. Charming scenery is presented as the boat glides up the now wider, now narrower, channel. On its banks the wealthy of Constantinople reside in beautiful villas during the hot season of the year. One of the first palaces met with is that of Abdul Hamid, the present Sultan, built close to the European shores. A fine variation of bills and valleys with gleaming villas and well-kept parks succeeds each other up to Rumili Hissar, or Roumelian Fort, on the European, and Anatoli Hissar, or Anatolian fort, on the Asiatic shore. These mighty ruins are fortresses built by Mahomet II in 1452 on each side and at the narrowest part of the Bosphorus, in order to force contributions from all passing vessels. The castled walls and the battlements of these ruins are the most picturesque to be seen anywhere. The boat made many stops, and at the last one, we could see the mouth of the Black sea through an opening in the mountains, where the Black sea disgorges into the Bosphorus. The flow of waters at the narrow portions of the channel is very swift. Many a luckless vessel in times gone by, and even steamers in our day, are irresistibly swept upon the hidden rocks by the strong current and concomitant winds. No wonder ancient lore has woven around this narrow stretch of water many myths of dangers encountered by the first navigators. Through this passage Jason and the Argonauts beat their adventurous way to Colchis in quest of the golden fleece. Here Xerxes and Alexander crossed with their armies, bent on their schemes of conquest. As we returned Bujukdere, Bekoe, Kandili, and Skutari successively glided by at our left.

Arrived again at the new bridge and having taken a Turkish dinner, we pushed through some of the narrow streets along the Golden Horn on the Stambul side. Here we encountered some of the old-time scenes of Turkish life: crowded streets, tumble-down sheds full of skulking dogs, open sewers in the middle of the lanes, swarthy Druses, Arabs and Turks, lounging around with their nargilehs or lazily at work. On turning round a corner we suddenly heard a great shout and beheld a crowd of ragged men, gathered around a scaffolding near the water and each one holding in his hand the end of a rope dangling from a high pole. The ends of each rope were fastened to a thicker one running over a pulley attached to the pole about thirty feet high. The other end of this thick rope was tied to an iron weight lower down. This iron weight was now resting on a pile which was to be driven into the ground.

Suddenly there was a universal shout from the motley assembly, and each one began to pull at his rope, thus slowly raising up the iron weight between two guide posts. Louder the shouting, higher the weight rose, until the overseer gave a signal. Then with one final yell each ragged Turk let go his rope. The heavy weight jerked up the tangled maze of rope ends as it descended with a thump on the head of the pile. Triumphantly the overseer measured how far the pile had been driven in and found it — a half inch lower. The real situation dawned upon us, it was no May festival, it was a pile-driving bee. Those thirty-five men were having a grand huzza about every fifteen minutes, while they raised the weight for one more half-inch blow. This manner of pile-driving was so ridiculous to us, that I could not keep myself from shouting and huzzaing with them, when after ten minutes they renewed their glorious achievement. Riddle: How long would it take these men to drive the piles needed for one of the Chicago skyscrapers? Yet what is time to them? Were they not earning enough for at least one pillau a day?

Finding that the Aiwan Serai, where the old city walls begin, was farther off than we had expected, we hired a boatman to row us up the Golden Horn. What a maze of old ramshackle boats and of ruinous huts along the banks! These riverbanks almost resemble those of Canton, which we had seen three months before. Half way up we passed an iron church. It is very tastefully put together and quite large, though not so large as that of Manila. From Aiwan Serai the old city walls run over hill and valley to the banks of the Marmora sea, seven miles distant. Istambul or ancient Constantinople, which this wall encloses, is built on a tongue of land formed by that sea and the Golden Horn. Two different walls, and for a portion of the distance, three different walls, were built parallel to each other in various periods of the history of Constantinople. The oldest and strongest was constructed by Theodosius in the sixth century, while the other two were added as outer defenses by the Moslems. A deep fosse ran along the outside, parts of which are now filled up or used as vegetable or wheat patches. Trees grow on the old ramparts, sheep and goats clamber among the debris of the falling walls. In places there are wide breaches in the three walls, which give a view of the city inside. A walk of three hours brought us to the Golden Gate, all of marble, but walled up.

Through this gate in 1452 the Mussulmen entered Constantinople, putting an end to the Greek empire. There is a superstitious belief that the Christians will again enter through this gate and end the Moslem dominion. No doubt it is possible that the Christian nations will again open this gate; but how foolish it is to suppose that walling up this gate will keep them out. There are breaches in these walls large enough to let whole armies sweep through, and a moderate-sized cannon could beat down the old walls anywhere.

Not far from this gate are the Yedi Kule, the seven towers, which adjoin the Marmora sea and form the end of the wall. They are part of a former fortress and palace of the Sultans. Now all is in ruins and only four of the seven towers remain. The Sultans were wont to confine their prisoners in these towers, and when it pleased them, also the ambassadors of Christian nations. The old keeper showed us the dark vault which the gracious Sultans used to reserve for the accommodation of the Christian ambassadors. From the top of the largest towers a fine view is had of the city and of the wide expanse of the Marmora sea. Through the kindness of two priests, that just then happened to join us, we were informed of the dummy railroad train just about to start for the city from the nearby station. It afforded us a chance to see Stambul also along the shores of Marmora and the Bosphorus, so that we had made a complete circuit of the city in one afternoon.

CHAPTER XX.

In the Meshes of a Stamboul Dragoman — Seeing Mosques — The Hamals — From Kuleli to Adrianople — A Hearty Welcome with the Resurrectionists — Through the Bazaars — Across European Turkey to Salonica — Pandemonium of Carriers — Shadowed by the Law — Stroll through New and Old Town — San Dimitri — Cutthroat Custom Rules — Off for Greece — Practical Hints.

Our first place to visit next day was old St. Piedro on one of the side streets near our hotel. It contains a painting of the Blessed Virgin by St. Luke. All of the picture except the face is covered with embossed silver. Near by is the orphanage of St. George, where we found German sisters in charge. The persistence of guides in pressing their services upon strangers is nowhere greater than in Constantinople. As we crossed the bridge to Stambul a dragoman joined us uninvited, and followed us so persistently, that I purposely pretended to understand neither French, English, nor German, in which languages he accosted us. We spoke Bohemian, which I had learned from my companion. But he followed us for a long time even to the museum in the Serai, for he saw that we were shamming. His persistence ended only when at last he was engaged as guide by an old gentleman whom we had seen at our hotel.

The most valuable and noteworthy objects in the museum of Stambul are the grand sarcophagus of Alexander the Great and the fine collection of gems recently found by Schliemann on the site of ancient Troy. The former is indeed a grand witness to the advanced state of the sculptor's art three centuries before Christ. The four sides of the sarcophagus represent, in images that seem to live and move, some of the battle scenes in Alexander's life, while its cover represents some scenes of his private life. Especially vivid is the hunting scene. The whole monument is wrought out of one large piece of red marble. Schliemann's collection gives a vivid insight into the affluence of the ancient Trojans, for it is a remarkable collection of precious stones and exquisite gold and silver chasing. In the upper stories, mummies from the Babylonian and Egyptian tombs are shown.

The tramways of Constantinople (and in a measure all over the Orient) are cumbersome and slow substitutes for walking, with an annoying system of paying fares. You must keep a slip of paper in your hand for the frequent inspection of a set of conductors, that board the car every few blocks to exchange places with each other. The car brought us to the Seraskian tower, the highest in the city, commanding an extensive view of Constantinople. Standing on its summit we were nearly blown off our feet by the violent north-wind, which was also quite cold. The Bosphorus, the Marmora sea, the Golden Horn, the aqueduct of Valens, the towers and buildings on the terraced hills of Galata and Pera, combine to form a magnificent scene. Here also one is impressed with the countless number of mosques in Constantinople. Each mosque of course has also its minaret to make it conspicuous. Immediately around the Seraskian tower is a vast public square, on the western side of which adjoin the administration buildings. The entrance to the buildings is by a high portal, from which the Turkish government derives the the name of Sublime Porte. Descending and strolling again through the bazaars, we had the usual experience with the boothkeepers. Desirous of getting rid of the importunity of one of them, who wanted to press upon me a silk scarf, I offered him one-third of the price asked. I was badly fooled; he eagerly accepted the offer and set about trying to sell some more of his goods. One of the loungers who lie in wait to steer strangers to the booths of their friends, followed us around the bazaar and afterwards through miles of streets, though we kept telling him that we would purchase nothing and had no need of his services.

On the stone approaches of a public building a group of Druse cobblers had established themselves with their few rude tools and pieces of leather. For the novelty of the thing, I allowed one of them to put new soles on my shoes. The work was done in twenty minutes and at small charge.

On our return from Galata our attention was drawn to a group of nine men, who were manœuvering around a huge wine butt. With its contents, it must have weighed three tons. Strong poles were slipped through nooses of the rope, which had been passed around the barrel. At a signal each of the hamals stooped to bring his shoulder under the ends of the poles, and at another signal, they rose, lifting up the butt with them. On they staggered up the hill, through the narrow streets, making a stop every forty or fifty steps. Hardly any wagons or carts are used for transportation in Constantinople, but nearly all is done by hamals or carriers. When we had paid our bills at the hotel, we had an example of what these hamals can do in the carrying line. One of them slung all our baggage on his shoulders, making use of his carrying strap, and on he walked across the Golden Horn to the railroad station in Stambul, a distance of over a mile. He stopped to readjust his burden only once on the entire way.

We were destined to have some vexatious experience before leaving Constantinople. A bevy of Turkish officials were sitting around a large table, at the railroad station, and demanded our passports before we should buy our ticket. We had intended to buy a through ticket to Salonica, with a stop-over at Adrianople in European Turkey. By detaining us until the last minute, they forced us to buy a ticket to Kuleli, thus mulcting us for almost double the real fare. The train was much crowded, so that we scarcely obtained seats, much less accommodation to sleep. There was a Jewish family who appropriated all the available room in our coupè. I soon left it therefore and improvised a bed in the passageway by means of a few valises and handbags. The country was uninteresting: a rolling prairie, sparsely settled. Farther on, darkness shut it out from view altogether. All the way to Kuleli junction, where we arrived next morning, and afterwards to Adrianople, the general character of the country remained unchanged. The rivers and creeks were much swollen on account of rain, which still continued. There are no farmhouses, like those in other countries. The tillers of the soil live together in miserable villages, preferring to walk a few miles to their work every day rather than be exposed alone to the depredations of roving bands. Very few are owners of the land they till: they are mere day-laborers for the rich landowners. Kuleli station is only a large wooden building, like a boarding house for railroaders in frontier countries. Here we took the train to Adrianople. The country hereabout must be fertile, but the soil seems to be put to little use. One is reminded of the western prairies of the United States. Here and there a wheatpatch was seen and a rude gathering of huts, a mere apology for a village. The railroad station is two miles from the city of Adrianople; why the only railroad should pass two miles from that important city of European Turkey only the perverse mind of the Turks might possibly explain. When we arrived, the rain was pouring down in torrents, and so the only sensible thing was to stop at the tavern near the station. Accordingly we passed a few hours here as best we might in the cold and damp rooms, waiting for the rain to stop.

The two-wheeled cart, which we took later on to the city, was certainly no improvement as to comfort. It swayed to and fro on the great flat boulders, that formed the pavement, throwing us from side to side without mercy. We landed at the Resurrectionist college, church and seminary. Both the lay brother, who received us, and the rector, Father Mosser, had lived for a time in Chicago. The rector had been a fellow student of Archbishop Feehan and was in correspondence with Bishop Muldoon. He prevailed upon us to take dinner with him, during which we learned some interesting facts about this part of the country. Adrianople was founded by the Emperor Adrian. The Turks made it their capital in European Turkey some time before the taking of Constantinople. This region was the scene of some heroic battles, being located at the junction of the Suma, Arda, and Maritza rivers and in the midst of a fertile territory.

Adrianople will no doubt yet play an important part in the history of Europe, when once Turkey will be parceled out among the Christian nations. The Russians are very influential in all that concerns politics and are steadily forging ahead. The "Young Turks" are becoming more and more numerous, especially in the European provinces. They wish to do away with the antiquated forms and customs of Mohammedanism, and foment opposition to the tyranny of Abdul Hamid. The most disagreeable feature of life in Turkey, the father told us, is the mischief which eavesdroppers and spies are able to do. One must be on continual guard not to say anything that can be construed as a censure of the government, though its rulings be ever so unjust and tyrannical. The fathers here, however, are well treated and have quite an influence in Adrianople. A number of Turks are converted to the faith every year, but the conversions from the Orthodox Greek church to the united Catholic Greek are not frequent: the people cannot be easily made to understand the difference between the Catholic and Orthodox churches. The papas are said to drive many of the people from the Greek church by their rapacity; most of these deserters join the Catholic church. The fathers hold the services according to the Greek rite, as most of the Catholics here are united Greeks.

The church is moderately large and nicely decorated. Like in all Greek churches, there is the iconostasis in front, which divides the sanctuary from the rest of the church. When the priest says mass, a curtain is drawn across the opening in the middle of the inconostasis and hides him from the beginning of the offertory to the end of communion. As a natural consequence most of the people leave before the end of the mass. Communion is given in two species, and the communicants stand while receiving. There are no confessionals in the church; the Greeks make an open confession of their sins to the priest and to the congregation. It is done within hearing of both. Fasting among the Greeks is much more rigorous and universal than among the Roman Catholics. There is such a mixture of nationalities in this congregation, that Father Mosser often has occasion to use eight different languages in one day.

After dinner Father Mosser went out with us in spite of the rain. From the top of an old fire tower we had a fine view of Andrianople. Most of the narrow and crooked streets are concealed by fine shade trees, which is certainly something unusual for a Turkish city. The

Maritza and its two forks, the Suma and Arda, join to make one large stream on the outskirts of the city. The Selim mosque of Adrianople was extolled as being equal in size and splendor to the Ahmed mosque in Constantinople. Inside, on each side of the mihrab, at the head of two high stairs, are two small pulpits, for reading the Koran. In the extensive bazaar and in the main streets, the merchants and the people looked trim and businesslike. But the sloppy weather soon tired us in our stroll and we were glad to get back to the station-tavern for an early sleep, as we were to take the train to Salonica at two o'clock in the morning.

For once there was no trouble with our teskere on boarding the train and we were again rolling through the dark fog and rain over a hilly country. Some stalwart natives were in the car with us; though belonging to the common people, they were polite and well behaved. Towards noon we had entered a more mountainous country. Glimpses of the Mediterranean showed through breaks in the hills. The seashore town of Deodadegatch glided into view a few miles to our left. As the train wound into the Maleka mountains a vast rock plateau loomed up to the right. The weather had worn the high cliffs into square blocks, that looked like the towers of a city. The sun had in the meanwhile driven off the rain clouds, giving additional charms to the wild scenery. Presently the train flitted through several tunnels and swung around into a wide and verdant valley, which stretched away in front like a vast road cut through a mountainous country. Far in the distance, at the farthest end of the valley, the light of the evening sun gleamed from the lake, around which the train emerged into a more open, though not much more settled country. At nine o'clock we arrived at the torch-lighted station Salonica, the ancient Thessalonica.

Here we again fell into the robber hands of custom

officials. Though we had not left Turkish territory, they scrutinized our teskere. Finding them in order, they began to scatter the contents of our satchels. They gave no heed to my loud and uncomplimentary remarks. They would probably have given some attention to them if they had been in a language known to them. The unlucky Baedeckers of my traveling companions were again yanked out in triumph and retained. They are probably the best-read books in Turkey, that is, if they really examine them as they claim. What a supreme stupidity of these Turks, to withhold such a well-known book under pretense of examining its contents for the ten-thousandth time! No arguments as to their harmless-ness would satisfy these blockheads or rather thieving scoundrels; and we put ourselves in serious danger of being arrested in trying to recover them by little less than force. We had to leave them in their hands with small hopes of getting them back in time for our departure from Salonica.

And now under the flare of the torches began the pandemonium of hotel runners, hack-drivers and their hangers-on. With one fell swoop they pounced upon the few Europeans, who made their exit from the station, almost tearing them to pieces like a pack of wolves, in order to secure a prize for some hotel, or a customer for their carriage. After obtaining some kind of terms from one of the runners, we were quickly brought to hotel Colombo, where we had no reason for complaint in regard to prices or accommodation. Supper was quickly served and well enjoyed by us, for very little chance of refreshment one has on Turkish railroads. As the town seemed to be yet full of life, we afterwards concluded to take a stroll through the streets. We were much amused by the antics of a night-watchman. Pass-ing the gate of an iron picket fence, we stopped to look at the building behind it. While we stood there a watchman across the street gave a signal by thumping his staff on the stone pavement. This was answered by another of his tribe farther on. Unsuspecting we continued our stroll to the market, where many torch-lights cast around a lurid glare. Unknown to us, however, we had been shadowed by the suspicious watchman and we were soon made aware of it, when we stood in a dark corner to watch the lively scene. For there was our watchman and four soldiers surrounding us at a distance of about ten steps and watching our every motion. We kept up the fun purposely for a while, lighting the cigars which we had bought, and pretending to examine the door of an old building where we stood. They were evidently at a complete loss what to think of our motions. Nor did they leave us until we had traversed quite a number of streets.

The inhabitants seem to be a pleasure loving people, for the cafés and taverns were well filled and music resounded everywhere. To our own hotel was annexed a beer-garden, (or rather a raki-garden), which was well patronized. In the background a large open stage was occupied by a band of Bohemian girl-musicians, such as are often found in southern Europe. At the end of each selection played, one of them went around with a plate, collecting voluntary contributions. Others would glide off the stage to lavish the charms of their conversation on those willing to receive them. Salonica seems quite cosmopolitan as regards nationality or language, for we heard several different languages spoken around us.

The Catholic church is in the neighborhood of the hotel. It is a spacious structure, newly built. As it is the only church in Salonica for Catholics, the fathers are obliged to preach in half a dozen languages. After mass a German father invited us to breakfast. Later on, our guide of yesterday hunted us up to show us some of the sights of Salonica. The business houses along the quay look somewhat modern, probably because business is mostly in the hands of Greeks. On one end of the quay is an old fortress and beyond some very fine residence quarters. Between them and the Jewish quarters is the old church of St. George, serving as a mosque. The entire interior is covered with mosaics, but the Turks are letting the building go to decay. A still older church is that of San Dimitri. It dates back to the second century, being no doubt the oldest building originally used for a Catholic church in Europe. Of course the Turks have possession of it and are letting it fall to ruins. A hungry-looking hadshi opened the ancient portals in order to show us the building. Two rows of granite pillars, all battered and chipped, rise about halfway to support the blackened timbers of the roof. The upper part of the church has the appearance of being the open trusswork of a foundry roof, so much dirt has blackened the timbers; yet the building seems to stand firm and solid. In the rear under a dark vault, the Moslem showed us a stone slab, full of dirt and candle drippings. He said it was the grave of San Dimitri.

Saint Demetrius was a martyr of the second century. It is easily possible that his body once rested under that dirty stone in the ruinous vault. But what connection had Islamism with a man who died for Christ and the Catholic religion? What reason had this ragged and untidy Moslem to show us his grave as something to be venerated? None other than the hope of bakshish. They are willing at any time to take over a consignment of Christian saints and pretend to hold them in equal veneration with their fraudulent prophet, if they promise to bring a harvest of bakshish. We left the gaunt keeper of San Dimitri in a somewhat flurried condition, for he had imprudently aroused our displeasure by his fanatic bigotry. Why should this ragged Moslem forbid us to to step on the dirty shreds of carpet? Or why should he deem our feet more unworthy to tread on the pavement of a stolen Christian church, on which he and his ragamuffin brother Moslems passed over at will? If he expected a double bakshish, he should have dispensed with some of his nonsensical formalities.

On calling at the custom house for our books we found it closed. It was Friday, and how could a giaour expect a Moslem to stir on Friday? The police superintendent merely expressed his sorrow for his inability to procure them for us. We fared no better at the American consulate. The consul could not speak intelligible English and I had to do business with him in French. We were mulcted two dollars for a visè of our pass: the Turk fines you for coming into his country and fines you again for leaving it. The American consul in our case was the collector of this outrageous taxation. We had to leave a few more dollars in order to obtain the promise of sending the Baedeckers on to Patras, Greece, as soon as they could be recovered from the custom house. The advantages of being an American citizen were far from being self-evident to us in Salonica.

Our runner brought us notice that a freighted steamer was to leave for Volo in Greece at five o'clock and that we might obtain passage in her. We packed up in a hurry and rushed to the quay. The steamer was lying out in the harbor among many other vessels. The custom house officials were on hand to examine our teskere: it seems the first thing these beggars would do in rescuing a man that fell into the water, would be to examine whether he had a right to fall off a Turkish quay without paying bakshish. The last Turk, who made an assault on our pocketbook was the boatman. Without much regret we shook the dust of the land of bakshish and teskere from our feet, and turned our faces toward the classic shores of Greece.

PRACTICAL HINTS. Unless the saving of time is of very great importance, travelers from Palestine, who wish to see Constantinople and Greece, will do well to take one of the coasting steamers at Jaffa. The large passenger steamers generally make no stops except in Athens, Smyrna, and Constantinople. The smaller ones will pick up freight and passengers all along the coast of Asia Minor and at the islands of the Aegean sea. Without any extra expense, and not a great consumption of time, the traveler will thus see many interesting places. Those that wish to have no annoyances at landing or during railroad travel in Turkey, should have their passes in order. No doubt a bakshish slipped into the hands of the officials would cover up a multitude of neglect in many places, perhaps everywhere. But the risk of being detained of course in one place or the other is ever present. Wherever any custom examinations are expected, a few silver coins will work wonders anywhere in Turkey; they always expect donations. Many travelers prefer to submit to the imposition, rather than be annoyed or detained. The morality of giving such bribes hardly comes into question; for the laws which cause this kind of annoyance, especially in regard to passes, are most unreasonable and infringe on the natural rights of travelers. Besides, the practice of bribing officials in Turkey is almost legal and serenely tolerated.

CHAPTER XXI.

On the Shores of Thessaly — Volo — Delaying
a Steamer — A Lively Lieutenant — Past Classic Scenes — The Piraeus and Athens — Ruins
of the Stathion and the Acropolis — The Parthenon — Lively Gatherings — On the Elysian
Fields — Scrambling about among Historic
Ruins.

The Roumania was a Belgian steamer and Captain
Coppens had his share of troubles with the Turkish harbor officials. There was a lively discussion about some
formality between a bevy of these ne'er-do-well Turks
and the officers of the ship as we boarded her. However the captain had a summary way of dealing with the
noisy blusterers: he hustled them off into their boats
and started the machines agoing. The Turks had done
us a good turn without knowing it; if they had not
detained the steamer, we would have come too late. As
the heavily laden Roumania swung slowly out of the
harbor, the departing sun shone from the white buildings and the hillsides of old Salonica. Later on, as
the vessel held its course southward through the Aegean
sea, the starry night held peaceful sway over the quiet
waters and phantom shores of Thessaly to our left. . Our
captain was quite a jovial fellow and made us feel quite
at home on the Roumania. As there were no cabins
for passengers, he arranged sleeping places for us on the
soft cushions of the dining-room seats. While sitting
with him and a couple of the officers in the dining-room,
he related some of his experiences on the Mediterranean,
nor was he backward in offering us other good things

to gladden the heart of a guest. He seemed well pleased to have some Americans and a priest aboard.

Early next morning we found ourselves in the Gulf of Volo, heading for the town of Volo, the ancient Jolcas. Wooded mountains arose on the shores of the gulf and islands around, and peaceful villages nestled at the water's edge. Volo is a lively town, spread along the curving harbor. Since the railroad connects it with the interior of Thessaly, a new addition has grown up, which is larger than the old town. A half a year ago the passport nuisance was abolished in Greece, so that we had no difficulty in landing at any of its ports. On inquiry at the railroad station, we found the schedule of trains rather inconvenient, and so reluctantly gave up an excursion to the mountains of Thessaly.

On a hill of the old town the open market presented a lively scene in the bright sunshine. On Saturday all kinds of petty merchants gather here, who spread their wares on rude tables under awnings or on the bare ground in the open air. The merchandise exposed for sale was mostly such as is used in the households of the common people. Good natured crowds moved up and down between the rows of stands. Most of them were dressed in modern fashion, though there was a sprinkling of such as were dressed in a mongrel European and Turkish garb, or in ancient mountaineer style. The mountaineers wear kilts, something like the highlanders in Scotland, only the kilts are made of white muslin and voluminously plaited. These dresses are so short that they reach only up to the knees, and make the sturdy men look like ballet dancers. The legs downward are often bare, or covered with leather lacings, which run up from the sandals.

Seeing some Greek taverns, we concluded to try a meal in one of them. A crowd of men were standing at the wine counter, much in the fashion of our American bars. The rest of the room was taken up by rude tables, on which the customers were served with eatables from the open kitchen in one corner. The place resounded with jokes and laughter and animated conversation. As strangers we attracted curious glances. Those present readily entered into the fun of the situation, when I tried some of the Greek, which I had studied on board ship. The new Greek, which is in use now, differs considerably from the Greek of colleges, especially as regards the pronunciation of the letters. There are two or three participial constructions which are foreign to ancient Greek, yet it would not be so hard for any one who has not neglected his Greek at college altogether, to familiarize himself with the new language. At the end of our short stay in Greece, I could make myself tolerably well understood. The Greeks who gathered around us at our table, spoke in high praise of the United States, and in the same breath they gave expression to their hatred of the Turks. The wine and fare pleased us very well, though it was of the simplest and served up in the most unsophisticated manner.

Proceeding along the beautiful quay to the new town, we heard that the steamer Paeneios was about to leave for the Piraeus of Athens. As we conjectured that we had seen the most interesting part of Volo and opportunities of departure would probably be scarce, we hastened to tranship our baggage to the Paeneios and to become one of her passengers. When we were as yet only a short distance from the shore, one of the steamers began to throw up clouds of black smoke and slowly move away. Our boatman gave us to understand that he feared it was the Paeneios. Frantically we shouted and waved our hats toward the departing steamer in order to induce it to wait for us. But no one seemed to notice any of our signs. It was just as well; on rowing a little farther out into the harbor, we found that the Paeneios was still listlessly lying at anchor. There was plenty of time for us to embark.

We had not purchased any tickets ashore and I inquired from one of the passengers about the price of passage. I was much surprised, when the purser came around to collect about twice as much as some of the other passengers had paid for their passage. I stoutly refused to pay more than the rest. He began to storm and rage and called up a few of the crew. The captain of the vessel also came up to add to the fracas. Partly in French and partly in Greek he gave me to understand, that the steamer was kept waiting on our account. The situation was getting to be humorous. I told them they need not detain the steamer on my account: I would pay what the rest of the passengers had paid and no more. I was getting curious to find out what these storming Greeks would do, and how long they would delay their big steamer in order to get the paltry advantage over us. As if they could not easily force us to pay the bagatelle by retaining some of our baggage at Athens! Three or four sailors grabbed hold of my arm several times in order to eject us by force. But somehow or other, a threatening look and a peremptory command not to touch me, though given in emphatic U. S. idiom, always made them desist. Finally the purser compromised the matter by saying, that the persons I had pointed out to him had gotten their tickets cheaper by mistake, and that they too would have to pay up the balance. As I did not want to make others suffer by prolonging a joke, I acquiesced and promised to pay about two-thirds of what he had asked. We had detained the steamer about twenty minutes, and gradually the passengers, who were all Greeks, had gathered on deck around us to see the issue.

A bevy of Greek army officers seemed to have enjoyed the fun as much as ourselves, especially a young lieutenant, by the name of Karras. He hovered around me during the entire voyage, asking a great many questions about the United States, and giving me much information about the interesting scenery through which we passed. The Greek of which I was capable was of course very defective, but we managed to make out each other's meaning. In the course of the afternoon we traversed the gulf of Volo, entered the narrow channel of the Negropont, or ancient sinus Euboeicus, headed round the northern end of the island of Euboea, and passed the Thermopylae. Towards evening we approached ancient Chalcis, at which harbor the vessel stopped during the greater part of the night. We were continually within sight of most picturesque mountains on both sides, and many a town passed in review, both on the mainland to the right as well as on the shores of the island of Euboea, the largest in the Aegean sea.

Lieutenant Karras woke me early in the morning to call my attention to the city of Chalcis, nestled at the foot of the mountains in a spacious bay. The island of Euboea runs parallel to a great part of the eastern coast of Greece. Between it and the mainland are the Talanta and the Euripo channels. As we issued from the last named channel into the gulf of Petali, the group of the Cyclades islands came to view in the south. We were soon able to distinguish the islands of Nio, Tino, Sertho, Naxia, Andro, Zea, Syra and others of classical renown. On the mountain heights to our right gleamed the white pillars of ancient temples. Then we passed Laurion, on the lower shores of Attica, and soon the headlands of the Peloponnesus rose ahead of us. Our vessel veered to the northward into the gulf of Aegina, passing the island of Aegina and Salamis to the left.

The shores of Attica to our right formed a gradual slope up to the mountains behind the city of Athens. About six miles inward the white temple of the Parthenon on the Acroplis loomed up. Behind it lies Athens, and above it are seen the surrounding mountains of the Parnassus, the Pentelicus, and the Immittos. About six miles south of Athens is its harbor, the Piraeus, being at the north end of the gulf of Aegina. The Piraeus harbor is completely landlocked, excepting a narrow passage. Quite a number of ships were at anchor. A new town has sprung up around the harbor, and the whole has an air of enterprise and business, to which one is not accustomed after coming from Turkish countries. We had no trouble in establishing ourselves in one of the suburban trains that run to Athens. Among the most noted of the pleasure resorts along the road, is the Phalerae garden. Its drives, walks, and summer houses were swarming with the gay crowds of the pleasure-loving Athenians. In Athens we took lodgings at the hotel Kamphaxes, where we had fine accommodations at moderate prices. A guide, who had joined us at the railroad station, but whom we had refused to engage, waylaid us at the entrance of the hotel, waiting until we should come out.

Though we told him several times, that we were out merely for a walk, he followed us up to the great square de la Constitution in front of the royal palaces and gardens. Athens is to a great extent a modern city; the architecture of the buildings, even the smaller ones shows a remarkably fine taste and the streets have a neat and tidy appearance. One side of the place de la Constitution is faced by the royal palaces. In front of these is a terraced public garden, full of luxurious trees and shrubbery, divided by tastefully arranged walks. The other three sides are lined with large hotels and public buildings, which enclose the spacious square or piazza. Crowds of people taking their Sunday outing filled the square. Rows of tables were placed at some distance from the cafès and restaurants. Our self-constituted

guide urged us to sit down at one of these tables
and order some refreshments, with which we not un-
willingly complied.

At a small distance to the rear of the palaces are the
Olympic exposition grounds, where the Americans
some years ago took away so many prizes in the Olympic
games. The grounds border both banks of the classic
Illyssus, which is merely a small, now mostly dry, creek,
running through Athens, and near it are the remains of
the ancient Stathion. It is a vast race-course in the
form of a long quadrilateral with rounded corners, surrounded on all sides with many tiers of marble steps or
seats. The Sakkas brothers have by their magnificence,
restored about half the seats of this Stathion. On this
arena the ancient Olympic games of Athens took place.
At the upper end still stand some columns, which record
the deeds of the champions of old. The grounds on this
side of the Illyssus are laid out in beautiful parks, where
among other monuments, stands also that of the poet
Byron, the great admirer of Greece. Behind and to the
left of the Stathion the columns of the famous temple of
Jupiter peer over the trees. A modern exposition hall
stands on a hill overlooking the park and the Stathion.

The open space around the exposition building was
swarming with gay crowds, either sitting at tables or
promenading about. Whole families were enjoying the
open air and listening to the artistic performances of a
band of musicians, paid by the city. The ladies appeared
in very tasteful costumes and the gentlemen rivaled them
in elegance of appearance. The features of the better
class of Greeks are well proportioned. On the whole I
have not seen such well-dressed and fine-looking people
anywhere else. The manners of the Greeks also struck
me as especially pleasing. On the way back to the
hotel our guide induced us to witness a play in a theatre,
which I did not find very interesting, probably because I

could understand only the drift of the plot. Of course it must have been much more interesting to my companion, for he fell asleep in the first act. The hotel people showed themselves very attentive to our wants, and we were therefore well pleased with our first experience in Athens.

Next day, after celebrating mass in the Italian church, our objective point was the Acropolis and its ruins. Passing the place de la Constitution and thence a few more narrow streets, we reached the approaches of the rocky cliff called the Acropolis. An iron picket fence surrounds the approaches and a small fee is collected at the entrance. Passing the ruins at the foot of the hill, we proceeded at once up the rocky sides to the propylae, or colonnades, which line both sides of the passage up to the Acropolis, and are part of the Sacred road, or Agia Ode. This road led from the temple of Eleusis, near Salamis, about seven miles away, to the doors of the Parthenon on the plateau of the Acropolis, and as the rocks fall off quite precipitously, a passage had to be cut through to the top. On one end of the propylae still stands the small temple of Victory, which has been restored from the heap of ruins to which it had been reduced by the ravages of centuries.

Up this stony and steep passage, and between graceful colonnades of the propylæa, the glorious pageant, formed according to the mysterious rites in the temple of Eleusis, annually wended its way from the Elysian plains. Thence the priests and priestesses in their chariots proceeded along the plateau to the great temple of Athens, or the Parthenon, drawing after them the thronging multitudes to witness the conclusion of the sacred rites. Often, no doubt, the overflowing crowds could not be contained in the Parthenon and would fill the rocky plateau, the Erechthion to the left, and the old Pelasgian temple, the oldest of them all, aside of it.

In our times of course no such gathering takes place. Bands of curious tourists climb this hill in order to admire the beauty and grandeur still lingering about the crumbling ruins. But let us try and obtain some kind of a picture of that celebrated hill as it looks to-day. Having reached the upper end of the propylæa, the whole of the rocky plateau lies before you. It seems about eight hundred feet long by five hundred wide, and an irregular quadrangle in shape. Old fortification walls run around the edges of the cliff, enclosing the whole. To the right of you, at about four hundred feet distance, rises the Parthenon, the most renowned temple-ruin of classic times; to the left are the much smaller ruins of the Erechthion and the Pelasgian temple. In some places the rocky plateau is strewn with fragments of carved rocks; but the most valuable of these are gathered and preserved in the museum, which lies on the farther end and to the right of the plateau.

After this general view of the Acropolis, let us proceed to a more close inspection of the ruins. Most of the pillars of the propylæa are still standing, but the frieze above them is missing in several places. On one side of the propylæa, on a projecting cliff, stands the restored temple of Victory, while the four walls of another structure occupy the corresponding projection of the rock on the other side. Proceeding toward the left near the middle of the plateau we come to the Erechthion, a small temple, almost square and minus its roof. It is especially remarkable for the Caryatides, noble statues of virgins, bearing on their heads the roof of a portico at its rear end. Five of these pillars still carry the frieze, as they have done now for over two thousand years, and these exquisite sculptures have been the admiration of many generations of men. The front of the Erechthion, which is on the side opposite to the propylæa, is adorned by exquisitely graceful Corinthian pillars. Behind them is the main wall of the temple, half fallen to pieces. Adjoining the Erechthion are the remains of the Pelasgian temple, the oldest of them all. It is merely a heap of stones, above which some of the old walls project, so that its size can be well traced. It is worthy of notice because it antedates all the other ruins by seven or eight hundred years, for this temple was erected by the first settlers of Greece, the Pelasgians. The walls that encircle the plateau are remains of fortifications built in the Christian era, though in many places they rest on foundations laid by the ancient Greeks.

The crowning glory of the Acropolis and of Athens, however, will always be the temple of the goddess Athenæ, called the Parthenon. The ground on which it is built is somewhat higher than the rest of the plateau. The platform of solid marble forms an oblong twice as long as it is wide. On the four sides of this platform rise the vast fluted Corinthian pillars and, parallel to them, an inside wall. The wall and the pillars support the low pitched roof. Under the eaves upon the pillars rests the exquisitely carved frieze or cornice, which on the ends of the two side walls of the temple widens out to form the low triangle of the front gable. This front, which faces the propylæa, is the only side which is still entire. The sculptures above the frieze in the front triangle are the admiration of all lovers of art. The friezes all around the temple in the time of Alexander were covered with plates of beaten gold, and the dazzling rays of the sun were cast from this golden crown on the summit of the Acropolis far and wide over the surrounding country. The whole structure is of the whitest Pentelican marble. In the middle of the temple stood the statue of Athenæ. But only insignificant traces of the treasures of art in and outside of this temple remain. The ravages of time and the neglect and vandalism of the Turks have destroyed most of the works of art, which the munificence of Cimon and Aristides and the art of Phidias and Ichthinos called into existence on this plateau.

The Turks, about a century ago, made use of this temple as a storehouse for ammunitions of war. A spark falling into the powder magazine resulted in a fearful explosion which tore off the entire roof, except a little part of it on the south end, destroyed the side walls, and overthrew the pillars in the middle of the two longer sides. But the broken rows of pillars on each side and the still perfect rows in front and in the rear even now give the exquisite outlines of the temple as it stood in the zenith of Greek glory. Each one of these vast fluted Corinthian columns, aspiring gracefully to the entablature, is a thing of beauty forever to the student of art. The secret of the beautiful proportions of this temple lies in its outlines, which are so arranged as to correct the faults of the perspective, inherent to the human vision. From whatever side or position the beholder views the structure it will always give the impression of perfect proportion. Thus it happens that these pillars, which look so straight and seem to stand perfectly perpendicular, are not really quite straight and are not standing perfectly perpendicular. They were so constructed and placed as to correct the diminution which the upper parts necessarily suffer, in the perspective of the beholder as he stands on the ground. What modern ingenuity has invented in order to correct the aberration of rays in photographic lenses, the Greek architects have done for the beholder of this temple in adapting its outlines to the perspective of the beholder.

But let us pass again through the propylæa and descend on the pathway to the left. We come to the immense arches of an extensive wall built of dark stone; it is the theatre of Herod, and is built at the foot of the hill. More ruins of Roman times are spread about in this neighborhood. On the farther end is the theatre of Dionysius or Bacchus, leaning up against the steep rocks of the hill. The proscenium and tiers upon tiers of marble seats rising in a semicircle and exquisitely carved, are still standing after two thousand years of exposure.

We obtained a plentiful meal in a nearby tavern at ridiculously low prices, and then continued our excursion and sight-seeing. Next to the Parthenon the great temple of Jupiter near the Stathion is the most renowned ruin of Athens. The Roman emperor Adrian has left many proofs of his munificence in all parts of Greece, especially in Athens, and this temple is one of the most noteworthy. At the entrance to the temple-grounds is Adrian's arch. It rivals in size and beauty the arches of Titus and Constantine in Rome. On the open grounds behind it are seen the great pillars of the temple of Jupiter. The roof of this temple was carried by fifty-six Corinthian pillars of vast proportions. Only a few of these pillars are still standing, while some are lying in fragments on the ground in the same position as they fell. The sections are six feet in diameter, about seven feet long, of Pentelican marble, and were so closely joined to each other that no seams are visible in the pillars that have not fallen. The platform, which formed the floor of the temple, is yet entire, and on one end of this platform a group of these pillars rise to a height of sixty-five feet. The temple of Jupiter was begun in the year 467 before Christ and finished by Adrian in the year of our Lord 147, a building period of 614 years.

During the rest of the afternoon we visited the tower of the winds, one of the oldest monuments of Athens, the ruins of the Roman forum, and the cemetery on the Elysian or Holy Road. In this cemetery, gravestones and monumental statues that were put up in the time of

Pericles and Themistocles, can yet be seen. Later on we paid our visit to the national museum. It contains any amount of statues from ancient times in a state of greater or less preservation. The most notable are the statue of Minerva from the chisel of Phidias, the Laocoön group, and the god Apollo. Many other relics of ancient times, too numerous to describe, are preserved in the spacious buildings. As the rain interfered with farther movements, we preferred to spend the rest of the day at our hotel.

CHAPTER XXII.

Through the Straits of Corinth — Amid the Cloud-swept Ruins of Acro-Corinth — Perennial Founts — The Vine-clad Hills and Shores of Achaia — Patras and Olympia of Old — Vast Fields of Olympian Ruins — On the Ionian Sea — Corfu and the Coasts of Epirus — Across the Adriatic — Practical Hints — Important Appendix.

Next day we had set apart for a visit to the ruins of Eleusis, about seven miles distant, and situated on the bay of Lepsina, opposite the island of Salamis. This excursion includes at the same time a drive over the Agia Ode, (Holy Road) through the greater part of the city, and through the beautiful plains that stretch away to the bay of Salamis and to the mountains. The Holy Road crosses over the plains southwest of the city and enters the defiles of the mountain-spurs near the shores of the bay of Lepsina. Having passed the hills, it winds in a wide sweep around a bend of the shore to the ruins of Eleusis. Extensive excavations have been made on the site of the ancient temples, where the Eleusinian mysteries were performed. The ruins lie to the right of the road at the foot of a hill on which stands a small Greek chapel. About an acre of ground is covered with fragments of statues, pillars, and carved stones, etc., that once were part of the many buildings, now fallen to ruins. The excavators have laid bare the foundations of most of the temples, so that they can be pretty well traced.

The oldest relic is the Pelasgian temple of Pluto,

which was only a small enclosure in the front end of the deep cave of Pluto in the side of the hill. Around this old Pelasgian temple many additions had been made in the course of centuries. ·The latest of them is the ˄ temple of Adrian. Part of the colonnade, which led from the Pelasgian temple to the place where the Eleusinian mysteries were celebrated, is still to be seen. Rows of marble seats, running partly up the hill in a semicircle; mark the mysterious quarters of this temple-complex, where none but the initiated were ever allowed to set foot, and where in later times the orgies of Dionysius or Bacchus took place. At the farther end of the ruins, old Roman fortifications rise out of the waters. Beyond the summit of the hill is an ancient temple, still under roof, though 2,000 years old. It is used as a museum, where a large collection of broken statues and fragments from the neighboring ruins are collected. The best preserved relics are a Venus, a Bacchus, and a Ceres. From the top of the hill the eye scans the Eleusinian fields.

The remainder of the afternoon we spent in visiting once more the Acropolis and its immediate surroundings. Adjoining the hill of the Acropolis, opposite to the propylæa, is the hill of the Areopagus. Its rocky summit is excavated in many places, showing the remains of the public buildings. On the declivities of the Areopagus, farthest from the propylæa, lie many acres of ruins where the streets which portioned off the squares are still traceable. On the other side of a deep ravine is the hill of the Nymphs. The ruins of a large temple and dwellings adjoining it are quite extensive. Here the priestesses of Minerva resided in olden times. The remains of the great monument of Philopapos crown the top of another bill, a quarter of a mile to the left. The temple of Theseus is not far from the Ode Agia, on the southern outskirts of Athens. It is the only one

THE ACROPOLIS

RUINS OF OLYMPIA

besides the one just mentioned which is yet under roof and entire. It is in the same style as the Parthenon on the Acropolis, though much smaller and without the fine proportions and exquisite ornaments peculiar to the Parthenon. The Corinthian pillars surrounding it are still standing.

In order to make the entire circuit of the Acropolis, we returned by way of the Areopagus to the west side of the Acropolis hill, opposite to the theatre of Herod mentioned above. This whole western side of the hill is occupied by old fortification walls. They overhang the cliffs above and abut on the sides. Soon we were entangled in a maze of narrow passages between old ruins and small huts, where the poorest Athenians have their abode. The passages were mere paths running up and down the cliffs halfway up the Acropolis. The lights of the city began to gleam below us and we were getting somewhat anxious. We would not have found our way out of this labyrinth, if one of the urchins had not come to our aid and led us through steep ravines and through the old walls of ruinous huts to the street below. We were glad to be again in the well lighted portion of the city. For a diversion we went for an hour or two to the hippodrome or circus, for which the Athenians have an extra building. The performances were of an inferior kind, except those of one of the riders, who atoned for the rest of the company and the stale jokes of the clowns. On the whole, however, we regretted the loss of an hour's sleep, which we might have enjoyed instead of sitting on the hard benches of the hippodrome.

Having missed the morning train for Corinth, we were obliged to wait till noon. While we were waiting for our breakfast at the restaurant, funereal music resounded through the drizzling morning air. A regiment of soldiers, who seemed rather of small stature and who kept rank and step but indifferently, presently marched through the sloppy street. Behind them followed a procession of black-robed papas and other mourners, chanting a mournful song. The hearse was exquisitely decorated with a profusion of flowers. It was the funeral of a Greek papa or priest. Next after the hearse came about two hundred of the cavalry and many civilians in carriages.

Our bill at the hotel was moderate. We were well pleased with Athens and its inhabitants. The train to Corinth was crowded, but we managed to get a seat near the window, and so were enabled to enjoy the beautiful scenery along the road. After passing Eleusis and the island of Salamis, the railroad skirts the gulf of Aegina up to the narrow isthmus of Corinth. The sun had in the meanwhile broken through the rain clouds, and shone brightly over the limpid waters to our left and the varied mountain scenery to our right. Like a snake the train wound along the rocky cliffs of the abrupt seashore, high above the blue expanse of the sea and the wave-worn, rocky beach. Our train crossed the deep canal, which now connects the waters of the Corinthian gulf on the west with that of the Gulf of Aegina on the east. Though the canal is only seven miles long, it is a remarkable engineering feat on account of the great depth to which it had to be cut into the solid rock. As we passed over its iron bridge, it seemed only a small creek in a deep abyss. Beyond lies New Corinth, in the province of Morea, the ancient Peloponnesus.

The present town of Corinth is built about five miles from the old Corinth and nearer to the water. Old Corinth was situated at the foot of a vast rocky cliff, some four miles from the shore. Only a small gathering of miserable huts, built upon hills of ruins, mark the site of the ancient city. As it was yet early in the afternoon when we left the train, we at once hired one of the clumsy country stages to bring us there. Very little of the ruins are visible, for they lie buried twenty or thirty feet below hills of debris and accumulated soil. Fields of grain and pastures now meet the eye, where the city once stood. Great excavations have been made and were then in progress on the outskirts of the village. Fortunately the foreman, who was directing the excavations, spoke English and kindly volunteered some information regarding the ruins recently uncovered.

They were the remains of ancient temples, that had been built over and around the perennial fountains, so often mentioned in the classics. The greater part of a large hill had been removed. Twenty feet below the surface, the foundations of temples, the intricate systems of conduits for distributing the waters of the fountains through the large complex of buildings and, under the walls of an old temple of the time of Pausanias, the Perennial fountains had lately been discovered. Four of the seven bronze lionheads, through which the waters gushed forth, still protruded from the old walls. Some distance from these excavations the rock-hewn caves over the fountain of Glaukus had also been brought to the light of day. The only monument of antiquity which had been visible before any excavations were made, were the remains of a Doric temple. It must have been stood on a considerable eminence, which explains the fact that it was not buried beneath the soil like the rest of the city. All that remained of it are three Doric pillars standing on one corner of the temple platform. They are at least three thousand years old. The dark granite, of which they are hewn, is crumbling away from age and the temple floor is covered for the most part by a drift of sand.

The great mount to the south of Corinth is called the Acro-Corinth. Its rocky cliffs, rising perpendicularly two thousand feet above the plain, are crowned by fortification walls, perhaps the most picturesque in the world. This stronghold dates from the Venetian occupation in the twelfth century. I wished to ascend to the summit, though the foreman of the excavations party thought that I would not be able to find the way alone, and that I would not have time before nightfall to accomplish the journey. Nevertheless I started out to climb the intervening hills toward a ridge, that seemed to afford a gradual ascent half way up the east side of the mountain. Having reached the place where the ridge meets the sides of the Acro-Corinth, progress seemed at an end, for I stood before an almost perpendicular ascent of broken rocks, and the fortification walls were yet at a great distance above us. Only by using hands and feet and reaching out for overhanging roots and projections, I wound gradually higher and higher around the south side of the mountain. Nearly exhausted I reached the plateau inside of the walls. The fortification walls enclose about a half square mile of uneven ground. Near the center, on an eminence, were the ruins of old temples, and on the summit was a wooden platform, which must be of recent construction, probably for scientific observations. From this platform there is a magnificent view of the surrounding country. The gulf of Corinth seemed like a slender arm of water, stretching inward from the Adriatic as if to caress the smiling landscape. The sun was casting its mellow evening rays over the hills and mountains on both sides and behind the Acro-Corinth. The fort has long since been deserted and in many places the walls are falling to pieces. On the side facing old Corinth the walls are particularly strong. Tar had been recently smeared on the edges of the turrets and walls and then set afire. It must have been a fine spectacle from below to see the edges of this great cliff encircled by a flaming crown in the darkness of the night.

I was fortunate in finding a path leading through the

gate in front and down the declivity outside, for it would have been impossible to climb down the same way which I had used in coming up. I found my traveling companion sitting with a few Greek villagers and a German, drinking wine at the tavern and having a good time. Dusk had settled over the land, when we again took our places in the conveyance. I was so fagged out by the steep climbing, that I fell asleep on the way. There was no life in new Corinth. The streets were not even lighted, and there was absolutely no business except in one tavern. What else was there to do, than to betake ourselves to rest at an early hour?

Early next morning we boarded a train for Patras. The train was crowded. It seems the Greeks like to travel. This also gave me a better chance to make use of the Greek which I had picked up with the help of a grammar in the last two weeks. The common people easily overlooked my mistakes and difficulties in trying to make myself understood. The conductor of the previous day was also on this train; he was a jovial blade, and often appeared at our window to exchange a few words with us. The train follows the shores of the Corinthian gulf, affording beautiful views of blue water on the right and mountain scenery to the left. The slopes between the gulf and the mountains form almost one continued vineyard from Corinth to Patras. At one place the mountains approach close to the shore, and a great headland impends over the railroad track, as if ready to fall into the sea. Several thriving towns are lined along the road and seashore, half concealed by trees and gardens. We found the Greeks social and friendly throughout, not overbearing, contented and happy, though most of them must be poor.

Across the bay of Corinth, which is only a few miles wide, picturesque chains of mountains rise and at last taper out into a headland opposite Patras. We arrived at

Patras at about three o'clock and took our headquarters at Hotel Anglia. Patras is a large town full of business and pleasure, both of which seem natural in such a fine port and in the midst of so luxurious and fertile a country. The tasteful buildings, the clean streets, the public squares and parks, cannot but make a favorable impression on the visitor. The variation of wooded hills and verdant valleys makes its surroundings a veritable paradise. Our first care on arriving was to inquire at the custom house for the unlucky Baedeckers, which we had requested the rapacious officials of Salonica to send on to this town. They were not there. They arrived several weeks later and the custom officials at Patras were kind enough to send them on to Rome at their own cost. Our cabman took us on to the Greek church of St. Andrew. It is built in the Greek or Byzantine style and very finely decorated inside. An old gray-bearded papa showed us the tomb of St. Andrew in the right aisle of the church. The lower part is of polished marble, inlaid with precious stones. Above it rests a canopy on four pillars. The tomb does not contain the body of St. Andrew, but after we had gained the confidence of the priest, the old man brought a gold and silver reliquary, which he said contains the thumb of the apostle.

Not far from this church is the public park overlooking the seashore. In the centre of this park, under a glass house, is preserved the mosaic floor of an old temple, which formerly stood there. It is one of the most artistic and largest floor-mosaics of ancient times in existence. Nobody that visits Patras misses an excursion to San Gerokomio, a very old Greek church and convent, a few miles south of the town. From this eminence the white buildings of Patras, encircled by the vine-clad hills and the blue sea beyond, formed a charming prospect in the mellow evening sunshine. As our carriage neared the convent it passed through idyllic gardens. Delightful shady bowers shield from the sun, and the fragrance of flowers and fruit fills the air. Near the entrance to the convent stood a modest wine tavern, where the rustic benches invite to rest and refreshment beneath the shade trees. The church and convent offer nothing particularly remarkable, except their age. Services were going on in the chapel, at which a score of finely dressed people assisted, standing in groups on the stone pavement. The services consisted of the usual drawling and interminable chant of Greek worship, while every now and then one of the clerics went around incensing his colleagues.

We had seen and heard the same thing often enough in Jerusalem, so we preferred to sit under the shade of the trees to listen to a few tunes of a wandering musician, who was playing on his harpsicord in front of the tavern. When we again entered the town after sunset, the streets were literally alive with well dressed, happy people chatting and laughing, while taking their evening promenade. The well to do were tastefully dressed, and this is especially true of ladies. There seemed to be quite a spirit of companionship and fraternity between the different classes. In one of the by-streets we came upon the ruins of an old Roman theatre, built of brick. The proscenium and stage and the great semicircle of terraced seats are still in good preservation. On the hill behind the city could also be seen the frowning walls of an old Venetian fort. The ancient monuments here and everywhere in Greece are strictly guarded; as well against the ravages of time, as against the vandalism of visitors. Otherwise there would soon be no relics left.

The Catholic church in Patras is in charge of an old Italian priest. It is in the business part of the city. He very urgently invited me to return and hold services on Sunday; but after returning from Olympia, I found that our boat would leave on Saturday. In the evening we attended an Italian opera in one of the gardens. It was all about an eccentric rich man, who was beguiled by a lot of monks (Latin monks of course) to buy some statues of women, to help their monastery out of financial difficulties. My traveling companion was soundly asleep before the play was half over, for he was partly deaf, and thus could not hear a word of the play or the fine singing. But when to his continual nodding he added a nasal solo crescendo pocc'a pocco, the surrounding Greek beauties began to cast around dimpled smiles to find the extra basso of the occasion. He of course remained unconscious both of their bewitching smiles and their youthful giggling. I was loath to wake him, for he was tired, and awakened would not be able to enjoy the fine points of the situation, one way or the other. It was worth something to me to be able to enjoy two comic operas at the same time. I merely nudged him once in a while to prevent fortissimos. Before the play was over I too had hankerings after the arms of Morpheus, whose soft embraces we went to enjoy at about eleven o'clock, though the streets were yet full of life.

Early next morning the train was taking us along the coast toward Olympia in the south of the Peloponnesus. Once more we were in crowded cars, passed the fruitful vineyards, conversed with pleasant people, and met the smiles of the same jovial conductor at the car window. At one of the stations my companion had gotten off to purchase some small article, and as his deafness prevented him from hearing the signal, he was left behind. I did not notice his absence, until one of the passengers reminded me of it. Hastily I informed our friend the conductor, though we were already a half mile from the station. He stood by us in our time of need and gave the signal to stop the train. In the meanwhile my friend had started to run after the train, but had given it up, when I jumped out to look for him, After some delay he was landed safely and our train sped onward. I don't expect to meet so good natured a conductor in the near future, especially not among the train czars of the United States. I suspect even our Greek conductor could not be so easily induced to delay a train so long, for any other than Americans. We arrived at Olympia about noon-time. It is situated in a verdant valley, watered by the small river Alpheios and surrounded by charming mountain scenery. The station is some distance from the excavations and the town consists only of a few houses, two rival hotels, and a museum near the great excavations.

After a scant dinner, we sallied forth to the ruins and their surroundings. The sharp cones of a wooded hill rose behind our hotel across the Erymanthos creek, which empties into the Alpheios near the ruins. It is the Kronion, commanding a fine view of the Olympian fields spread below. We tried to gain its summit, which is of considerable height, but after a futile attempt desisted on account of the thick growth of underwood. From its southern base extend the great excavations a quarter of a mile square. Nearly fifteen feet of rubbish and soil had covered this space. But the patient labor of the excavators had now disclosed the vast ruins to the light of day. Here lay the remains of temples, playhouses, baths, arenas, treasure vaults, that once had attracted the champions of the world, and the countless thousands of spectators even from distant Rome. The walls are now heaps of stones, the pillars are lying in confusion on the ground or over each other, the ornaments and carvings of the buildings are scattered in fragments between the huge blocks of stone foundations. The great temple of Jupiter is near the centre. Its huge platform foundation is still intact and some of the Doric pillars are still standing. On one side are the remains of the arenas and the playgrounds, surrounded on all sides by the ruins of the apartments for the participants in the games.

On the other sides are the intricate mazes of the Roman thermæ or hot baths, the foundations exposed, the pillars broken off or toppled over, the underground conduits laid bare.

All the glory of the Olympian games has departed. Over these grounds, how many thousands were not wont to throng in ancient times at the call of the envoys. Every four years they were sent out to the four quarters of the compass to invite the Greek and the Barbarian to take part in or to witness the deeds of far-famed men! How many a heart exulted in victory on that stathion, in the throwing of the disk, in wrestling or running, in poetry or song! How many also departed vanquished and sick at heart, broken in despair, themselves and their friends ruined by the lost wagers! There shouts of applause uprose and fired the contending champion to renewed exertion; there also the sharp tongue hissed words of scorn and derision at some defeat. Fiercely the storms of envy and ambition often raged in the hearts of the champions, rousing up kindred storms in the hearts of the spectators, that vented itself into shouts of rage or exultation at defeat or victory. All is silent now, the shouts are hushed as in a grave, the games died out, the crowds are dispersed ages ago. Nothing except the hesitating step of the curious tourist resounds on the place, his vacant stare and wondering remark, mingled with the gasconading swagger of the guide, have taken the place of all the glory of the Olympiads.

A suspicious watchman follows you around from afar, lest you are ridiculous enough to abscond a piece of crumbling marble as memento. No doubt the watchman was found to be necessary in order to preserve the heaps of ruin, for it is remarkable, what absurd things travelers will often burden themselves with in order to show to their friends that they have visited places of note. We left the grounds on the road which leads up to the museum on the hill. A bridge here leads over the Eryman-thos. While we crossed over the bridge, a boy, aided by a noisy dog, drove a straggling herd of goats along the creek bottom; this is the only crowd of living beings that still hover around Olympia now. The museum is filled with carvings found on the excavated grounds. The most notable piece is the statue of Hermes and child, by Praxiteles, and the great Nike or goddess of victory, which stood on the apex of the large temple of Olympia. Along the walls were the great groups of marble figures that adorned the triangular friezes of the temple. They represent the battles of the Centaurs with the Lapidæ, and were restored from the fragments of the statuary found in the excavations. The figures are of gigantic size, and the two groups are each over one hundred feet long. The parts missing are filled in with plaster of Paris casts, so that the groups are quite complete. Before we went to rest, we sat for a while in the balmy evening air, on the rude benches of a primitive wine-tavern, talking to one of the natives.

The next morning we took the train back to Patras, and after vainly inquiring for our strayed Baedeckers, we leisurely established ourselves on board a steamer for Corfu and Brindisi. But the steamer tarried until ten o'clock at night. The next day the sun rose in splendor over the rippling waters. The verdant shores of Greece glided by to our right, while the island of Zakynthos, Cephalonia, and St. Maurice stood guard on the left. At about eight o'clock Corfu, or Corcyra, as the Greeks call it, hove in sight, and at ten we anchored in the harbor immediately in front of the town of Corfu. The city presents a pleasant view, with its palaces on the high promontory, the tall houses along the quay, and the mountains behind. As it was Pentecost day, we felt obliged to hear mass if possible. Services were just going on at the modest cathedral. A scant congregation was present standing in groups on the stone pavement of the church. It seemed to me that some of the ladies were more anxious to show off their fine dresses, and meet acquaintances, than to follow the services. The singing and music were excellent and appropriate to the holy sacrifice. Let no American complain of too frequent collections in their churches, for here we had no less than five different collections taken up during mass. Perhaps that was necessary, for the contribution flowed but scantily in every one of them. After mass we were shown a miraculous statue of the Blessed Virgin in one of the side chapels.

Not much of Sunday quiet reigned on the great square and in the crowded streets. Most of the stores were wide open. The houses and the vessels in the harbor were bedecked with numerous flags in honor of Prince Constantine of Greece, whose birthday it was to-day. After partaking of a delicious Greek dinner, we passed the rest of our time in strolling through different parts of the town. It struck me as peculiar that there should be so many stories to the houses. The south part of the town is built on a high promontory. A large portion of this is occupied by the old royal palaces and its surrounding parks and gardens. Here the king sometimes spends the summer months. The highest top of the promontory is crowned with fortifications built by the Italians, the former lords of the island. Through ancient barracks, still occupied by soldiers and kept in good repair, we climbed up the steep hill to the weather observatory. An old tower affords a charming view of land and sea. Eastward across the sea, on the mainland of Epirus, the convent of St. Salvator lay perched on top of a high mountain, and northward of it the Albanian mountains lined the shore. Beneath us the island of Corfu curved away from the mainland westward into the sea, full of picturesque scenery. South of us the open Adriatic gleamed through the studding island mountains. The old station keeper was highly gratified by a small fee for the use of his telescope. We returned on the romantic path to the town, and again boarded the Servia in order to continue our voyage to Brindisi and Naples.

PRACTICAL HINTS. For those who are acquainted somewhat with the ancient classics, Greece is one of the most interesting countries. They will do well to set apart for it a corresponding portion of the time at disposal for their travels. In a short time the knowledge of ancient Greek will enable them to become somewhat familiar with the present language, that is, if they have not shirked the study of Greek at college, and take some pleasure in having a chance to make the only practical use of it during their lives. The relics of ancient times are found all over. Greece will become intensely interesting, if the history connected with it is a little freshened up.

AUTHOR'S ANNOUNCEMENT.

"O'ER OCEANS" is to appear in four different series, independent of each other, yet forming a continuous narrative of a journey through both hemispheres, as follows:

FIRST SERIES: Chicago — San Francisco — Hawaiians — Japan — China — Manila.

SECOND SERIES: Singapore — Burmah — India — The Himalayas — Goa — Bombay — Cairo — Jaffa.

THIRD SERIES: Jerusalem — Palestine in Bedouin Garb — Syria and Islands of the Mediterranean — Smyrna — Constantinople — Athens — Corfu.

FOURTH SERIES: Naples—Rome—Vienna—Munich — Oberammergau — Switzerland — The Rhine; Paris — London — New York — Chicago,— supplemented by incidents of a tour of all the European countries, the north of Africa, and Canada.

On account of other much more important duties, the author can give but a very limited amount of time to the writing and publication of "O'ER OCEANS," and still less to other matters connected with their distribution. But their reception by the public has been very gratifying. Nevertheless, he wishes it to be especially understood, that the chief object of these books is to bring to the notice of the English-speaking world one of the most remarkable books *in any language,* the Spanish CIUDAD DE DIOS, of which he has undertaken the first English translation.

Reader, if you have been generous and intelligent enough to find some good points in this book of travel, in which I have sought to describe in a pleasing way the trivial incidences of a mere jaunt around this insignificant earth, what may you not expect in an intellectual journey through CIUDAD DE DIOS, where the hidden beauty of the universe is pictured in a manner superior to what has been spoken or written, short of direct and certified inspiration from on high; where he that will but reflect and is of good will, sees opened up vast vistas of light in confirmation of all that is true, all that is good, all that is noble and inspiring, in the history of the human race? Such a book is CIUDAD DE DIOS, the English translation of which is heralded by " O'ER OCEANS."

Series 9

CPSIA information can be obtained
at www.ICGtesting.com
Printed in the USA
BVHW04*1058170918
527708BV00014B/1403/P

9 780484 418935